Growing Up Urban

D1510865

Alexander J. Dunnbar
Dunnbar Press Publications

Published by:
Dunnbar Publications
BookSurge Publishing

First Edition: February 2003
Copyright © Carl S. Taylor 2004

Printed and Bound in the United States of America

Production, Layout and Cover Design
www.jktconsultants.com

ISBN: 1-4196-4817-9

To order additional copies please contact us at:
Dunnbar Publishing
www.cstaylor.org
www.thirdcity.org

Contents

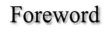

Foreword

Towards Social Justice for Urban Youth
Richard M. Lerner
Tufts University

As is true of all young people, urban youth are diverse, varying in interests, abilities, involvement with their communities, aspirations, and life paths. Unfortunately, this diversity has largely remained a hidden truth to many academics, policy makers, and even practitioners working in urban youth-development programs. All too often, the view of urban youth within developmental science, and the attitude of many policy makers and practitioners about these young people, has been framed by looking through a deficit "lens" that assumes that all these youth may be characterized as either "at risk" or as already engaged in problematic or health-compromising behaviors.

This view of urban youth sends a dispiriting message to young people, one that conveys to them that little is expected of them because their lives are inherently broken or, at best, in danger of becoming broken. This approach to the conceptualization of urban youth is also patently false. It is mistaken for both theoretical and empirical reasons.

The problems that do exist among some urban youth are neither inevitable nor the sum total of the range of behaviors that do or can exist among them.

7

Derived from developmental systems theory, a positive youth development perspective stresses the plasticity of human development and regards this potential for systematic change as a ubiquitous strength of people during their adolescence. The potential for plasticity may be actualized to promote positive development among urban youth when young people are embedded in an ecology that possesses resources and supports that offer opportunities for sustained, positive adult-youth relations, skill-building experiences, and opportunities for participation in and leadership of valued community activities. As *Growing Up Urban* richly illustrates, such supports exist even in those urban settings that many policy makers have abandoned as resource depleted or resource absent.

Empirically, research in life-course sociology and in life-span developmental psychology, as well as in developmental biology, attests to the presence of variation that is at least as great as inter-group differences. As explained in books, chapters, and articles by Carl S. Taylor, the eminent sociologist whose theory and research form the basis of the singularly important and timely approach to urban youth represented in *Growing Up Urban*, the more than two decades of community programs and associated scholarship involved in the Michigan Gang Research Project have demonstrated that positive growth-supporting actions may be marshaled in urban communities. Such actions result in nuanced and diverse ways in which the potential for positive development may be actualized among urban youth.

Professor Taylor and his co-authors do not deny the challenges facing urban youth, and in fact they present erudite and insightful analyses of the data that depict these challenges. However, the message of *Growing Up Urban* is not one of despair in the face of these statistics. It is a message of hope, one compelling derived from sound scholarship about and successful work in furthering opportunities for positive development among urban youth.

We learn from *Growing Up Urban* that the linkages between characteristics of positive development among urban youth and their contributions to their communities are varied but, within such diversity, lies the bases for understanding the range of positive potentials for healthy development that exists among these young people and the numerous ways in which one can promote their contributions to self, family, community, and civil society.

Professor Taylor and his colleagues allow us to understand that there are profound implications for policies and programs of the information presented in *Growing Up Urban*. If it is true that the strength and vitality of a democracy can best be ascertained by the treatment afforded its poorest or politically weakest citizens, then the vision in *Growing Up Urban* offers our nation a means to enhance social justice in new and deeply significant ways. Recognizing that urban youth have strengths and possess an enormous capacity for healthy and positive development legitimates new and sustained investments in the lives and communities of these young people.

The model for positive youth development found in the pages of *Growing Up Urban* is a clarion call for America to set out on a new path for providing opportunities for healthy development of urban youth. The demonstrated merit of the model followed by Professor Taylor and his colleagues deserves to be brought to scale and sustained across all urban centers of our nation. All citizens owe these pioneers in promoting the positive development of youth a great debt of gratitude for enacting a vision that will enhance the only true capital upon which the future welfare of America depends, the healthy and productive development of all of our young people.

Richard M. Lerner, Ph.D.

Richard M. Lerner is the Bergstrom Chair in Applied Developmental Science and the Director of the Applied Developmental Science Institute in the Eliot-Pearson Department of Child Development at Tufts University.

Acknowledgments

Acknowledgments

First and foremost, I thank God, for without Him this would not have been possible. To my family and friends, thank you for your support and patience. My undying gratitude goes out to everyone who collaborated on bringing this book to fruition. This book is dedicated to my family and friends.
Pamela R. Smith

Pamela R. Smith is Project Manager, African American Female Study, Michigan Gang Research Project, Doctoral Student, Department of Sociology, Michigan State University.

Let me first thank God for the blessings and the people He has placed in my life. None of my life's work would be possible without Him.

To my wife Jackie and my two children Matthew and Jennifer, you will never know how grateful I am for every day with you and how thankful I am that you are a part of my life.

To Carl Taylor, thank you for the opportunity to share my thoughts and opinions as part of your book. Working with you is a pleasure and an honor.
Randy C. McNeil

Randy McNeil is President of the Youth Sports and Recreation Commission, Detroit, MI

Thanks to the Creator for everything, I would also like to thank everyone who has supported us in this endeavor.
Virgil (Al) Taylor

Virgil Taylor, is a native Detroiter and currently serving as Managing Partner for Human Ecology Management.

My deepest gratitude and thanks to God, family, friends, co-authors and colleagues. I'm indebted to Dunnbar Publishing, JK Thornburg and Associates, Tina Louise Vivian, Wayne State University Department of Public Safety Chief Tony Holt, Wellington and Alexander Dunnbar, OTO Teams at Tufts University and Michigan State University.
Carl S. Taylor

Carl S. Taylor is Professor of Sociology at Michigan State University

Community Youth Leadership participant, DeVonta Harris, Coordinator, Judith Richmond and Michigan State University Extension Southeast Regional Director, Hank O. Allen

One

"Lots of people think if you're from the city you're different...different like bad, ugly, stupid."
Perry, age 15

Growing Up Urban

In these modern times urban children and youth are far too often negatively influenced and affected by factors in their community. Professionals and volunteers working with young people are frequently challenged by the negative influences. Historically, positive youth development methods and practices have been implemented in urban communities via the nuclear and extended family and through such institutions and organizations as block clubs, churches, recreational clubs, agencies and leagues and others. Today street culture is increasingly dominant, frequently supplanting the values learned by children and youth through traditional methods and programs.

For the past three decades street culture has become more dominant, its tentacles digging ever deeper into mainstream society as Madison Avenue and big business frequently embrace its "flava" for commercial appeal. In urban communities the rapid evolution of street culture has created a widespread negative impact on children and young people.

The normalization of ignorance and violence are the most obvious and detrimental elements affecting urban (and other) communities, and nowhere is this more apparent than with the children and youth. A wide array of activities attract young people in the new millennia, from sports and recreation to music and dance and an increasingly vast array of interests involving technology; modern young people are more and more diverse in their interests.

With this in mind it is of paramount importance that activities and new technologies are utilized at every opportunity to positively influence young people and help to counteract the increasingly pervasive negative influences of street culture.

To effectively do this, individuals working with children and young people in urban communities must understand the dynamics of street culture and how it impacts and influences every aspect of working with urban children and youth.

It is also important to note that in these modern times there can be an element of danger in working with people of all ages, it is therefore critical that the professional and volunteer alike be ever vigilant while performing the various tasks associated with their jobs or assignments. Far too frequently, people young and old will choose to resort to violence when they are angry or dissatisfied.

This model will address some methods for dealing with violent situations and scenarios but nothing replaces common sense, vigilance and attentiveness to potentially volatile situations. As often evidenced by television news programs and in media reports children are sometimes the target of enraged, disillusioned and/or mentally unstable adults. Violent assaults against children by parents, associates and lovers of parents and others have become more commonplace in news reports.

The professional and volunteer working with children and young people must be continually vigilant and aware of potential threats on properties where children are involved. The ability to quickly recognize a potential threat and act appropriately can literally mean the difference between life and death in extreme circumstances.

Two

"I love my hood, people think we're ghetto...that's our place, our hood, it's our thang."
Donny, age 20

Positive Youth Development
What Is It?

Positive Youth Development has existed in one form or another in all American communities throughout the history of the nation. In more recent years the need to better understand child and in particular adolescent development has lead to significant bodies of academic and scientific research and analysis regarding the early years of human development. The recognition of the need for positive support mechanisms for children and youth ultimately led to serious study within the academic/scientific community and thus the formal philosophy and doctrine of positive youth development was established.

While there are various approaches to what is now known as positive youth development one of the more widely known and accepted doctrines embraces a philosophy based on what is known as the... "40 Developmental Assets"

40 Developmental Assets

Search Institute℠ has identified the following building blocks of healthy development that help young people grow up healthy, caring, and responsible.

"EXTERNAL ASSETS"

Support

Family support: Family life provides high levels of love and support.

Positive family communication: Young person and her or his parent(s)communicate positively, and young person is willing to seek advice and counsel from parent(s).

Other adult relationships: Young person receives support from three or more non-parent adults.

Caring neighborhood: Young person experiences caring neighbors.

Caring school climate: School provides a caring, encouraging environment.

Parent involvement in schooling: Parent(s) are actively involved in helping young person succeed in school.

Empowerment

Community values youth: Young person perceives that adults in the community value youth.

Youth as resources: Young people are given useful roles in the community.

Service to others: Young person serves in the community one hour or more per week.

Safety: Young person feels safe at home, at school, and in the neighborhood.

Boundaries and Expectations

Family boundaries: Family has clear rules and consequences, and monitors the young person's whereabouts.

School boundaries: School provides clear rules and consequences.

Neighborhood boundaries: Neighbors take responsibility for monitoring young people's behavior.

Adult role models: Parent(s) and other adults model positive, responsible behavior.

Positive peer influence: Young person's best friends model responsible behavior.

High expectations: Both parent(s) and teachers encourage the young person to do well.

Constructive Use of Time

Creative activities: Young person spends three or more hours per week in lessons or practice in music, theater, or other arts.

Youth programs: Young person spends three or more hours per week in sports, clubs, or organizations at school and/or in community organizations.

Religious community: Young person spends one hour or more per week in activities in a religious institution.

Time at home: Young person is out with friends "with nothing special to do" two or fewer nights per week.

"INTERNAL ASSETS"

Commitment to Learning

Achievement motivation: Young person is motivated to do well in school.

School engagement: Young person is actively engaged in learning.

Homework: Young person reports doing at least one hour of homework every school day.

Bonding to school: Young person cares about her or his school.

Reading for pleasure: Young person reads for pleasure three or more hours per week.

Positive Values

Caring: Young person places high value on helping other people.

Equality and social justice: Young person places high value on promoting equality and reducing hunger and poverty.

Integrity: Young person acts on convictions and stands up for her or his beliefs.

Honesty: Young person "tells the truth even when it is not easy."

Responsibility: Young person accepts and takes personal responsibility.

Restraint: Young person believes it is important not to be sexually active or to use alcohol or other drugs.

Social Competencies

Planning and decision making: Young person knows how to plan ahead and make choices.

Interpersonal competence: Young person has empathy, sensitivity, and friendship skills.

Cultural competence: Young person has knowledge of and comfort with people of different cultural/racial/ethnic backgrounds.

Resistance skills: Young person can resist negative peer pressure and dangerous situations.

Peaceful conflict resolution: Young person seeks to resolve conflict nonviolently.

Positive Identity

Personal power: Young person feels he or she has control over "things that happen to me."

Self-esteem: Young person reports having a high self-esteem.

Sense of purpose: Young person reports that "my life has a purpose."

Positive view of personal future: Young person is optimistic about her or his personal future.

Applying the 40 Assets Model

To help people think about the range of possible asset-building acts, the Search Institute outlines the following six principles:

Everyone can build assets: Building assets isn't just about great families or schools or neighborhoods. It's about each person playing a role in the raising of our children.

All young people need assets: While it is crucial to pay special attention to youth who struggle economically, emotionally, or otherwise nearly all young people need more assets than they have.

Relationships are key: Strong relationships between adults and young people, young people and their peers, and teenagers and children are central to asset building.

Asset building is an ongoing process: Building assets starts when a child is born and continues through high school and beyond.

Consistent messages are important: It is critical for families, schools, communities, the media, and others to all give young people consistent and similar messages about what is important and what is expected of them.

Intentional redundancy is important: Assets must be continually reinforced across the years and in all areas of a young person's life.

Theory and Reality

There are significant challenges to be addressed and/ or considered in the application of any theory that deals with young developing minds and bodies. One of the most difficult and often perplexing aspects of dealing with children and youth in urban communities is recognizing and addressing the extraordinary influence of "street culture." The reality is that children and youth in urban communities routinely face a host of powerful negative influences that are most typically in direct conflict and opposition to positive developmental assets.

In addition to the various challenges associated with a rudimentary simplistic application of any theory is the safety and security component that must be considered when working in a potentially volatile or dangerous environment. It is naïve and could potentially even be dangerous to simply embrace the 40 Assets or any other child/adolescent developmental theory or model without consideration of the forces at work within a community. This is particularly true in urban communities where street culture has established a hybrid eco-system based on embracing, practicing, perpetuating and celebrating ignorance and violence.

It is noted that while many children and youth growing up in urban communities are at risk this does not diminish their potential for positive development nor their desire to grow into healthy, well adjusted contributing members of society.

What is critical is a deep understanding of the forces at work within a community, the tools necessary for combating the negative forces and an appreciation for the need to work wisely and safely to ensure the well being of the children and youth being served as well as the individuals working to assist them in their growth and development.

Three

"*Ever since I was little, I knew who the players were. Pimps, players or preachers, they all got game. Getting paid, nothing else matters...*"
Lonnie, age 19

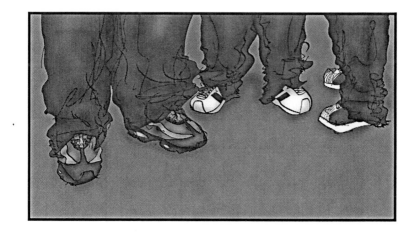

Negative Youth Development
What it is

In Urban America a phenomena has flourished over the past hundred years and become more prevalent since the civil disturbances of the 1960's and 70's and the proliferation of a drug culture. This under-recognized and frequently neglected phenomenon is what we call negative youth development. History is replete with stories and facts regarding the use, abuse, misuse and negative development of children and youth, so it should come as no surprise that street culture would be a perfecter and perpetuator of such practices.

In street culture, children and youth are at great risk of negative influence(s) without having to have direct exposure to those agents and elements that may actually pose a threat. Images delivered via television, radio, video games etc., are continually reinforced by the reality witnessed daily on city streets and in various neighborhoods. Many children and young people growing up in urban communities across America regularly witness drug dealing/using, criminal behaviors/activities, prostitution, random violence, homelessness, decay, deterioration, and other negative activities and/or conditions.

To further exacerbate the problem of bearing witness to such behaviors, activities and conditions many children and young people today are intentionally lured to participate in negative behaviors and activities. A common misconception is that all adults in communities and in some families have the best interest of children and youth at heart. There are in fact many adults that routinely utilize the abilities and even the age of a child or young person to more effectively conduct illegitimate and/or illegal business and practices.

For the child or young person growing up in a household where violence, criminality or other negative activities are taking place such things are normal. To assume that the child or young person growing up in such a household would find fault with the adults or activities within it is a ludicrous assumption at best. Early childhood and/or adolescent normalization and/or acceptance of ignorance and violence will typically give rise to a mutated and distorted sense of values.

When considering for instance the Forty Assets of Positive Youth Development model we must also consider that for many children and youth growing up in America there is a reverse order that exists. For every positive developmental asset there is a negative counterpart that is far too frequently imposed on developing young minds. For the child or young person that is being exploited by adults to engage in criminal or other negative behaviors the "role model" is often a negative role model. This does not suggest that the child or young person is always physically or mentally abused in the classic sense.

The exploited child or young person may in fact have more than adequate food, shelter and clothing. The negatively affected child or young person may feel loved, adored, admired, appreciated and respected based on their ability to perform according to the desires, wishes and needs of the influencing elder or elders.

Misunderstanding the relationship between a child or young person and an adult that is negatively influencing them provides the catalyst for trouble. Many well-intentioned professionals and volunteers make the fatal mistake of casting aspersions on individuals they know to be "bad influences" on children and young people they are working with. It is generally ill advised to cast aspersions on someone a child or young person may look up to as it can be disastrous if not dangerous to do so.

A research study (source: Michigan Gang Research Project) in a large urban city reveals a stark similarity between children in divergent urban groups regarding how they view parents and family members. Two groups of middle school aged children were selected for this study. The first group of young people (group 1) had never been in trouble (reportedly). Each member of this group attended private school and lived in a family where both parents were in the home. Members of the second group of young people (group 2) had been charged with either being incorrigible or having committed some criminal or egregious act. As result of their offending activities and/or behaviors these young people were subsequently in the juvenile justice system.

Every member of group 2 attended public school and lived in a single parent home.

The chart on the next page reveals that negative and positive influences affect both groups:

GROUPS 1 & 2 RESPONSE ANALYSIS

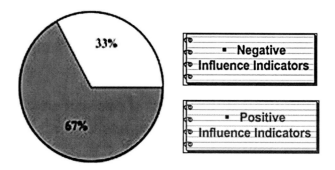

The following are eight of the questions asked in the survey:

1. Do you love your parents and other family members?

2. Does anyone in your family sell/deal or use drugs?

3. Do you ever wish you lived with someone else?

4. Do you know anyone in jail or in prison?

5. Do you want to be like your parent(s) when you grow up?

6. Do you think it's acceptable to commit a crime to survive?

39

7. Have you ever seen violence between members of your family?

8. Does any member of your immediate family engage in criminal behavior?

The following are the results of one section of the survey from the children interviewed:

	Question I	Question II	Question III	Question IV	Question V	Question VI	Question VII	Question VIII
Child 1	Yes	No	No	Yes	No	Yes	No	No
Child 2	Yes	No	No	Yes	Yes	Yes	No	Yes
Child 3	Yes	Yes	No	No	Yes	No	No	No
Child 4	Yes	Yes	No	Yes	Yes	Yes	Yes	No
Child 5	Yes	No	Yes	Yes	Yes	Yes	No	No
Child 6	Yes	No	No	Yes	No	Yes	Yes	Yes
Child 7	Yes	No	No	Yes	No	Yes	No	No
Child 8	Yes	No	No	Yes	Yes	Yes	No	No
Child 9	Yes	No	No	No	Yes	No	Yes	Yes
Child 10	Yes	Yes	No	No	Yes	No	No	Yes

Note: Group 1 is indicated in Gray, Group **2** is indicated in **black**.

Groups 1 & 2 Divergence Analysis

RISK INDICATORS   POSITIVE INDICATORS

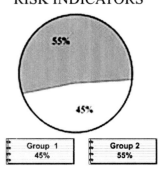 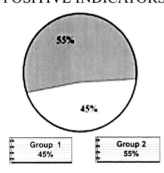

The analysis provided demonstrates the duplicitous nature frequently found in the modern urban community. While on the surface it might appear that there is an obvious advantage and subsequent risk reduction for the youth of group one, further analysis reveals that this is not necessarily true. Too frequently the assumption is made that the child or young person being raised in a two parent, "middle class" (group 1 type) home is not at risk. Conversely, it is often erroneously assumed that the child of a lower income class single parent (group 2 type) home is at higher risk.

Interviews with more than one thousand children and young people throughout four major urban centers have revealed that these common assumptions are incorrect. While the data supplied in the provided analysis can be interpreted in several ways, it is noted that with rare exception most urban youth in modern society are at some level of risk. The disadvantaged child, or the child that comes from an overtly dysfunctional family can seemingly be at increased risk and may require more attention and assistance than the child or young person being raised in what appears to be better circumstances. Research regarding urban youth culture reveals that it is imperative that professionals and volunteers working with urban youth recognize and understand the threats and perils that face children and young people in the modern urban community.

 Traditional surface observations are insufficient in modern child and youth development efforts particularly in the urban community. The child that appears to come from a well adjusted, two parent, middle class family might well be the child of a family involved in drug use or sales, criminal activity, domestic violence or other maladies that plague many families in America today. It is also noted that the child that comes from a family that suffers from apparent dysfunction might well be better adjusted than his or her peer(s).

The point here is that it is ineffective, inappropriate and insufficient to take surface views to be absolute when making determinations regarding the needs of children and young people.

The effective professional and volunteer will establish relationships with those children and young people they serve. Communication and continued observation are keys to success. Recognizing when the climate changes can result in the ability to avert disaster in the worst case scenario.

The following are a series of questions the professional or volunteer should ask themselves daily when working with children and young people:

- Is there any noticeable evidence of abuse (mental or physical)?

- Is there a noticeable sudden change in the appearance or behavior of a child or young person, or a group of peers?

- Are new groups developing that are demonstrating behaviors and/or attitudes associated with gangs?

- Is there any sudden change in the types of clothing being worn by a child or young person, or a particular group of young people?

- Is clothing being worn seasonally appropriate?

- Is a child or group of children being isolated, ignored, intimidated or ostracized by other children?

- Is there any obvious evidence of bullying?

- Does a particular child or group of children seem to hesitate when it comes time to go home, go to the restroom or at any other time where they might be isolated and that might subsequently put them at risk from bullies/predators?

• Are adults in the life of a child or young person prone to displaying violent, aggressive and/or inappropriate behavior?

• Is there any obvious evidence of drug and or alcohol abuse by parents or other older friends, relatives or siblings associated with a child or young person?

• Is there any evidence of domestic violence or the threat of domestic violence in the family life of a child or young person?

• Is there any evidence of sexual predatory activity regarding a child or young person?

This is a particularly difficult dilemma to address where young women and girls are concerned. Not withstanding the problem associated with young women, a different aspect of this problem has been revealed in recent years and that is sexual predatory activity where boys and young men are being victimized. Homosexual predatory activity has become a tremendous problem in the urban community.

It is recommended that the professional or volunteer pay close attention to behaviors and attitudes when working with urban youth. Modern urban youth culture is a blend of dynamic, fast paced, ever changing ideas, ideologies, theories, attitudes and concepts that has dramatic impact and influence on the minds, attitudes and behaviors of the modern urban, child, youth and family.

The successful professional and volunteer will pay close attention to the changing winds of the forces that constitute urban culture and youth culture so that he or she may adjust and adapt as necessary.

Many will argue that traditional methods are paramount to achieving success with young people. Urban youth culture does accept a certain portion of what it considers "old-school" but this acceptance should not be confused for "tradition" in traditional terms.

Four

"Safe in the hood, aight, safe is yo gat."

Youth Violence and the Urban Community

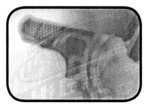

For the professional and volunteer working with children and young people it is imperative that an understanding is acquired regarding the harsh realities and facts pertaining to the potential for violence in urban communities. The ability to conduct effective threat assessments, quickly assess threat scenarios and have effective, efficient emergency plans is a necessary part of working in the modern urban landscape.

The effects of violence can have social and emotional effects. Wilson (2000) claims that urban youth who have witnessed high levels of violence experience significant negative consequences in their psychosocial functioning. Moreover, they suffer from higher incidences of substance abuse, school failure, anxiety, or behavioral problems in comparison to other children.

Consider the following facts about "Juvenile Gun Violence" documented in Combating Violence and

Delinquency: The National Juvenile Justice Action Plan (1996, objective 3):

A trend analysis of juvenile homicide offenses shows that since the mid-1970's, the number of homicides in which no firearm was involved has remained fairly constant. However, homicides by juveniles involving a firearm have increased nearly threefold. In addition, during this same period, the number of juvenile arrests for weapons violations increased 117 percent. When guns are the weapon of choice, juvenile violence becomes deadly (American Psychological Association, 1993; Howell, 1994; Zimring, 1986).*

Because recent crime statistics excluding homicides gathered by the Federal Bureau of Investigation do not show all chargeable offenses involved in a particular incident, there is no reliable way to determine how many crimes involved a weapon, what was the nature of any injury, or whether the crime involved illicit drugs. Therefore, it is difficult to determine the precise role that guns and illegal drugs have played in the recent increase in violent juvenile crime. Although there are gaps, the data make a compelling case that the role of guns in juvenile-related homicides is increasing at an unprecedented level.

*Citation was obtained from the U.S. Department of Justice, Office of Juvenile Justice and Delinquency Prevention (OJJDP), Combating Violence and Delinquency: The National Juvenile Justice Action Plan (1996).

During the period 1976 to 1991, firearms were used by 65 percent of juvenile homicide offenders (44 percent used handguns). Firearms were used in nearly 8 out of 10 juvenile homicides in 1991, compared with 6 out of 10 in 1976 (Snyder & Sickmund, 1995).*

Young black males have the most elevated homicide victimization rate of any race or gender group. Homicides involving firearms have been the leading cause of death for black males ages 15 to 19 since 1969, and the rates more than doubled in the decade from 1979 (40 deaths per 100,000) to 1989 (85 deaths per 100,000) (Snyder & Sickmund, 1995).* Teenage boys in all racial and ethnic groups are more likely to die from gunshot wounds than from all natural causes combined (Jones & Krisberg, 1994).*

Between 1979 and 1991, the rate of suicide among youth ages 15 to 19 increased 31 percent. In 1991, 1,899 youth ages 15 to 19 committed suicides, a rate of 11 per 100,000 youth in this age group. Firearms were used in 6 out of 10 suicides among youth ages 15 to 19 in 1989 (Allen-Hagen, Sickmund, & Snyder, 1994).*

---

*Citation was obtained from the U.S. Department of Justice, Office of Juvenile Justice and Delinquency Prevention (OJJDP), Combating Violence and Delinquency: The National Juvenile Justice Action Plan (1996).

51

In 1990, the Centers for Disease Control and Prevention surveyed a nationally representative sample of 9th to 12th grade students about the number of times they had carried a weapon such as a gun, knife, or club during the prior 30 days. One in 20 students indicated he or she had carried a firearm, usually a handgun. A number of additional surveys confirm an increased propensity among young people to carry guns (Callahan & Rivera, 1992).*

The increased availability of guns and access to guns by youth has had devastating consequences on schools and communities.

In many schools, learning is no longer the top priority; survival concerns lead many students to avoid school entirely or carry weapons for protection. Educators must divert attention from academics to monitor and control student aggression. In neighborhoods, people are apprehensive about going outside their homes, and fights that once involved fists have become deadly exchanges.

*Citation was obtained from the U.S. Department of Justice, Office of Juvenile Justice and Delinquency Prevention (OJJDP), Combating Violence and Delinquency: The National Juvenile Justice Action Plan (1996).

Juvenile Gun Homicides

Gun homicides by juveniles have nearly tripled since 1983,while homicides involving other weapons have actually declined.

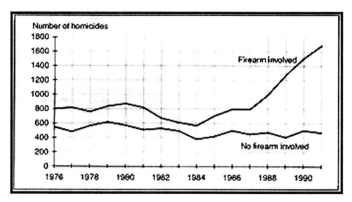

From 1983 through 1991, the proportion of homicides in which the juvenile used a gun increased from 55% to 78%.

Data Source: FBI. 1993 Supplementary homicide reports 1976-1991 [machine-readable data files].

Source: Snyder, H., and M. Sickmund. 1995 (August). Juvenile Offenders and Victims: A National Report. Washington, D.C.: Office of Juvenile Justice and Delinquency Prevention, U.S Department of Justice .

As evidenced in events over the past several year's youth violence has reached epidemic proportions in the United States. While the more widely reported incidents have occurred in rural communities the incidence of youth violence in urban communities is a routinely reported event.

"The exacerbation of youth violence in urban American communities is directly correlated to an increased sense of hopelessness and a belief that real opportunity does not exist among many urban youth" (Taylor, 2000).

Furthermore, in Combating Violence and Delinquency: The National Juvenile Justice Action Plan (1996, objective 3) "Youth Gangs" section:

Researchers have identified a number of factors that put youth at risk of gang involvement: poverty, school failure, substance abuse, family dysfunction, and domestic and societal violence (Spergel, 1995).*Easy access to illicit drugs and the perceived financial rewards of drug dealing pose attractive alternatives for youth with inadequate education and limited employment opportunities, leading them into high-risk behaviors and potential gang involvement. Gang recruits often have a poor self-image, low self-esteem, and little adult participation in their lives. Some of them are children of gang members and are choosing a familiar lifestyle.

Many are seeking the recognition they fail to receive from home or school. Even parents with strong parenting skills cannot ensure that their children will not become involved in gangs, particularly in low-income, problem ridden neighborhoods. Youth gang research has focused extensively on the gang-drug nexus. Recent research, however, suggests that there is also a significant connection among gang involvement, gang violence, and firearms.

In one study based on responses from 835 male inmates in 6 juvenile correctional facilities in 4 States, researchers found that movement from non-gang membership to gang membership brought increases in most forms of gun-involved conduct. Forty-five percent described gun theft as a regular gang activity. Sixty-eight percent said their gang regularly bought and sold guns, and 61 percent described "driving around shooting at people you don't like" as a regular gang activity (Sheley & Wright,1992).*

Additionally, experts report that gangs appear to be increasing their organizational sophistication and their propensity for individual and collective violence (Quinn & Downs, 1995).*

*Citation was obtained from the U.S. Department of Justice, Office of Juvenile Justice and Delinquency Prevention (OJJDP), Combating Violence and Delinquency: The National Juvenile Justice Action Plan (1996).

These structural and behavioral changes are often, but not universally, attributed to the impact of the drug trade and the availability of firearms. Another study indicates that gang homicide settings differ from non-gang homicide settings in that they are more likely to involve public areas, automobiles, and firearms, among other elements (Maxson, Gordon, & Klein, 1985).*

The researchers further speculate that location, automobile involvement, and gun presence suggest potential points of intervention.

*Citation was obtained from the U.S. Department of Justice, Office of Juvenile Justice and Delinquency Prevention (OJJDP), Combating Violence and Delinquency: The National Juvenile Justice Action Plan (1996).

Gun violence has become normalized in many urban communities to the point that it is widely recognized as the accepted method of dispute resolution in street culture. Further perpetuating the problem of gun violence among young people is the glamorization of extreme violence found in modern entertainment in the forms of music, movies and video games.

While some will argue the merits of research and theory regarding urban violence, prudence dictates that every effort is made to minimize the potential for violent incidence involving children and youth.

From the seminar "*Youth Violence in Urban Communities*" the following proposals were offered as solutions in decreasing youth violence:

- **Decrease youth access to guns:**
  Given the centrality of guns in recent homicide trends, continued efforts to decrease access to guns should be a primary goal.

- **Create community youth programs that address the social meaning of violence for adolescents:**
  Program developers should incorporate interventions that address the social meaning of violence for adolescents. In addition to

basic street survival, the social meaning of violence is tied to issues of respect, honor, and pride within peer groups. Interventions should offer alternatives that encourage non-violent conflict resolution and help strengthen mutual respect in interpersonal relationships among youth.

• **Increase adult engagement in the lives of children and youth:**
This can be achieved through efforts such as mentoring programs to link individual children with supportive adults; educational reform to improve teachers' ability to form meaningful relationships with students; and policy changes to support quality child care programs and allow parents more flexibility in juggling work and family issues.

• **Involve communities in designing programs to address youth violence:**
Community members are on the front lines of youth violence and should be involved in designing efforts to address it. Community members may know which young people are most at-risk and why. They may understand unique neighborhood characteristics and social dynamics that fuel youth violence. And they may be aware of local resources and leaders that can be employed to help

address the issue. Collaborative efforts between the police and community leaders can help to ensure that crime is abated in ways that reinforce residents' sense of security and mutual trust.

- **Encourage policies that focus on prevention:**
  Punitive policies that lower the age at which children can be tried as adults do not address the underlying causes of violence. While traditional criminal justice procedures are often necessary to ensure the safety of citizens, long-term solutions must include efforts to prevent violence from occurring in the first place.

- **Conduct further research and facilitate dissemination of best practice models:**
  More research is needed to better understand the causes and consequences of violence. For example, there is a lack of longitudinal research on the effects on children of exposure to violence. In addition, more evaluative research on prevention programs would help establish a set of best practice models that could be disseminated for adaptation by local communities.

Source: Youth Violence in Urban Communities: In The Urban Seminar Series on Children's Health and Safety (Wilson, 2000).

Combating Violence and Delinquency: The National Juvenile Justice Action Plan (1996, objective 3) offers information in reference to "Promoting Maturity and Respect for Life":

Developmental issues associated with a lack of maturity can contribute to youth violence. Young people seldom understand the full impact of their behavior (Pacific Center for Violence Prevention, 1994).*

This lack of awareness of consequences coupled with a tendency to respond with violence can be a lethal combination.

Prevention strategies that help youth to understand the impact of and take responsibility for their actions and that demonstrate ways to handle problems without resorting to violence can be highly effective (Shapiro et al., 1993).*

Such programs should be available to high-risk youth between the fifth and sixth grades, when violence-prone attitudes appear to increase and become entrenched.

*Citation was obtained from the U.S. Department of Justice, Office of Juvenile Justice and Delinquency Prevention (OJJDP), Combating Violence and Delinquency: The National Juvenile Justice Action Plan (1996).

Research has shown that in addition to the environment of fear in which many youth live, the culture of the illicit gun trade has popularized firearms and made backing down from arguments and "losing face" difficult for young people (Fagan, 1995).* Self-defense, the need to show off, or the need to ensure respect and acquiescence from others can also contribute to youth gun violence (Elliott, 1994).*

Other studies indicate that youth who respond aggressively to shame, who find guns exciting, who feel comfortable with aggression, and who believe that guns bring power and safety are most likely to engage in gun violence (Shapiro et al., 1993).*

Thus, prevention programs that promote self-esteem, respect for others, cultural pride, and nonviolent conflict resolution can be an effective antidote to the culture of violence (Henkoff, 1992).*

Adult programs focusing on parenting skills can complement youth gun violence prevention programs. Classes on gun violence and its impact on victims should be provided in juvenile justice programs, schools, and community settings.

*Citation was obtained from the U.S. Department of Justice, Office of Juvenile Justice and Delinquency Prevention (OJJDP), Combating Violence and Delinquency: The National Juvenile Justice Action Plan (1996).

Five

"Selling dope is a job. You got money if you sell dope."
Martel, age 14

Drugs and the Urban Youth

In urban youth culture drugs represent two major components of everyday life; enterprise and entertainment. In a series of interviews conducted with urban youth when the question was raised regarding drug usage, the response was consistent. Drugs are for suckers. To understand this ideology and how it does not seem to fit into the urban street culture landscape one must first understand that to the average urban youth (as with many youth throughout America) marijuana is not considered a drug. Secondly, hard-core drug users are typically viewed as losers that are to be exploited.

One of the lowest forms of existence in the urban community is that of a "dope fiend." If the dope fiend is such a lowly creature in the urban eco-system the obvious question is then why do their ranks continue to swell? The answer frequently given by youth in urban communities is that becoming a dope fiend is a process, only the weak fall victim to the scourge of serious drugs and thus when things go bad many weak minded individuals fall victim to dope and the dope dealer. For the industrious, serious and cunning individual these weak people provide a steady and solid customer base to be continually exploited.

As stated in Combating Violence and Delinquency: The National Juvenile Justice Action Plan (1996, objective 3) "Drugs and Delinquency" are a grave issue:

Researchers have not established a definite causal link between drug use and delinquency, they have confirmed a delinquency-illegal drug use correlation. In the 1987 Survey of Children in Custody, 81 percent of wards in State-operated institutions responded affirmatively when questioned about lifetime use of drugs (Krisberg, DeComo, & Herrera, 1992).*

Nearly half (48 percent) admitted to being under the influence of drugs or alcohol while committing the offense for which they were institutionalized.

Although there is some variance across offense categories, the percentage of institutionalized wards who reported being under the influence of drugs or alcohol at the time of the offense ranged from 34 percent in the case of rape offenses to 51 percent for robberies and 59 percent for drug possession.

*Citation was obtained from the U.S. Department of Justice, Office of Juvenile Justice and Delinquency Prevention (OJJDP), Combating Violence and Delinquency: The National Juvenile Justice Action Plan (1996).

Although the link between drug use by juveniles involved in serious delinquency and by those not attending school is well documented, drug use by another segment of the youth population not considered to be at risk students who have progressed to their senior year in high school also continues to be the focus of serious concern.

According to the results of a 1994 national household survey, monthly marijuana use among 12 to 17 year-olds nearly doubled from 1992 to 1994 from 4.0 percent of students surveyed to 7.3 percent following a steady decline in drug use from 1979 to 1992.

The survey also reported that 2 million youth rate themselves as heavy alcohol drinkers, with over 1 billion cans of beer being consumed annually by junior and senior high school students alone (1994 National Household Survey on Drug Abuse, 1995).*

*Citation was obtained from the U.S. Department of Justice, Office of Juvenile Justice and Delinquency Prevention (OJJDP), Combating Violence and Delinquency: The National Juvenile Justice Action Plan (1996).

 Marijuana is a recreational drug routinely used by many urban youth along with alcohol, the two frequently imbibed together. As a source of enjoyment, marijuana and alcohol are typical viewed as harmless with no correlation drawn between these two substances and drugs such as cocaine, heroin or other narcotic drugs. Another disturbing trend is the use of GSB as a recreational stimulant and sexual aide sometimes voluntarily taken by young females, other times administered to them involuntarily when drinks are "spiked."

A sinister form of entertainment associated with drug use and abuse is the sexual exploitation of drug users for entertainment purposes. It has become commonplace for sex parties to take place throughout the "hood" where drug addicts perform sexual acts in exchange for money and/or drugs. The sexual acts involved in these "parties" range from activities including group sex (gang bangs), lesbian and homosexual sex shows, bestiality, etc.

It is widely known that drugs are a readily available commodity in many urban communities. Knowing the landscape of the street will help the professional and volunteer working with children and young people in affected areas. When working in areas that suffer from the plight of drugs it is important to gain an understanding of not only the neighborhood/s but who the inhabitants are.

If a threat exists that poses the potential for harm to the worker, the volunteer or the children and young people being served then the problem should be addressed with the proper authorities.

Combating Violence and Delinquency: The National Juvenile Justice Action Plan (1996, objective 3) reports the following information about "Youth, Guns, and Drugs":

Drug activity appears to exacerbate juvenile violence in two ways. First, firearms are more prevalent around drug activity (American Psychological Association, 1993).*

In 1984, the United States saw a dramatic increase in juvenile gun homicide, coinciding with the introduction of crack cocaine into urban communities. Studies show that as the use of guns by drug-involved youth increases, other young people obtain guns for their own protection.

*Citation was obtained from the U.S. Department of Justice, Office of Juvenile Justice and Delinquency Prevention (OJJDP), Combating Violence and Delinquency: The National Juvenile Justice Action Plan (1996).

This cycle of fear or "diffusion" theory (Blumstein, 1994)* is supported by recent research on the "ecology of danger" (Fagan, 1995).* A 1993 Louis Harris poll showed that 35 percent of children ages 6 to 12 fear their lives will be cut short by gun violence (Louis Harris and Associates, Inc., 1993)*, and a longitudinal study of 1,500 Pittsburgh, PA, boys revealed that their frequency of carrying a concealed weapon increased when they began selling drugs (Van Kammen, & Loeber, 1994).*

The second way drugs and juvenile gun violence appear related is through the impact of drugs on a young person's perceptions. Adolescence is a time of taking risks and seeking stimulation, and juvenile delinquents report a certain level of excitement as well as fear of apprehension in the commission of a crime. Many youth revel at the thrill of roller coasters, some ignore cautions about "safe sex," and others seek an "ultimate high" from illicit drugs or possession of a deadly weapon.

*Citation was obtained from the U.S. Department of Justice, Office of Juvenile Justice and Delinquency Prevention (OJJDP), Combating Violence and Delinquency: The National Juvenile Justice Action Plan (1996).

Six

"I'm a man cuz I take care of my business. Taking care of yourself means you're a man."
Anwar, age 13

The Young Urban Male

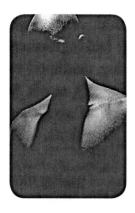

"The first liquor I drank, my first cigarettes, even my first reefers, I can't specifically remember. But I know they were all mixed together with my first shooting craps, playing cards, and betting my dollar a day on the numbers."

Source: Malcolm X: The Autobiography of Malcolm X (as told to Alex Haley, 1965) (p. 58)

Malcolm X describes here part of his indoctrination into street culture as a young man who had recently moved to a small urban community on the East Coast. Are drug and alcohol experimentation and gambling youthful rights of passage for many adolescent males? The answer is probably yes, but for the developing urban adolescent male they can be more than a simple experimentation phase, rather they can be and frequently are a requirement for acceptance and subsequently for survival in the "hood".

The challenges facing the young male growing up in most urban communities are inexplicable. The delicate balance that must be achieved for many young men growing up in urban communities where street culture is prevalent is tantamount to navigating a small boat through raging waters in a tempest. For the uninformed and uninitiated it can be nearly impossible to understand how difficult and complex the world of urban street culture can be. Some would dispel the accuracy and legitimacy of many facts that apply to achieving manhood as related to street culture. But one merely needs to tour the streets of urban communities throughout America to bear witness to the troubling facts.

It is true that there are many examples of young men that have managed to thrive and achieve some level of success, sometimes great success that have come from urban areas. Oftentimes these young men are from disenfranchised, disaffected, impoverished areas. The hard-core realities are that it is far more difficult for young men from "the streets" to not only thrive but to survive than it is for their suburban counterparts.

"The impact of the drug culture and violence on young black males is very depressing. When you realize the young ages of these young boys and men one can only sense that society is in a very serious dilemma... mind you not Detroit or Michigan, but American society."

Source: Brunetta Brandy, Attorney:
In Dangerous Society (Taylor, 1990, p.84)

The question frequently arises, what happened to cause the decline of conditions in urban communities, the answers are numerous and complicated. For the young male growing up in urban communities part of the problem has historically been limited access to resources and opportunities. Today resources for the disenfranchised and poor are perhaps more limited than at any other time since the beginning of the industrial age. The anger and resentment frequently manifested in the modern young urban male is part of a cycle that began long ago.

As evidenced in an interview with a young man from a large urban community, the challenges facing a young male growing up urban are many:

"I kinda like school, but it's hard to answer questions when you know that you might get got for knowing the answers. I mean, fella's in the crews they be watching and I ain't trying to get beat down just for answering some dumbass question. Besides, school don't really mean all that much, I ain't got no money to go to no college and I damn sure ain't gonna get no scholarship so what's the point in doing good? I mean I like to rap but I ain't no rapper, I can hoop a lil but I ain't got it like that to go to no NBA. I don't even know what I'm gonna do when I get outta school, ain't no jobs, I ain't no baller, I mean I might sell a lil weed but that's bout all. I ain't going in no damned army, that's for damn sure. I guess I'll just hustle like everybody else."

The sense of hopelessness expressed by this young man is far too typical of the views and feelings shared by many young males in urban communities.

An even more disturbing point of view was revealed in an America Undercover special aired on HBO. In the documentary titled Thug Life in D.C. (Levin, 1999) a young man in prison for shooting a police officer was asked what was the happiest day of his life. After pondering the question a moment, he slowly lifted his head and displayed a hideous grin. His eyes glistened as he seemed lost in thought before responding "the day I got my muthafuckin gun."

This young man was 18 years old at the time of the filming, 16 years old when he shot the officer. His happiest memory in his short life was the day he acquired a handgun. No mention of a particular day at summer camp or any mention of a special Christmas or Birthday… the day he got his gun! As the program continues and he is interviewed further he reveals that as a young man growing up in his neighborhood he knew that he wasn't the brightest, the biggest or the toughest… he was however known for being the "craziest" and that gun equalized everything for him, made anything possible for him, in his "hood" What he could not gain through skill, knowledge, cunning or even brute strength could be gained through the use of that gun.

It is noted that Laura Bush, the First Lady of the United States has recognized the need to address the numerous challenges facing young urban males in America. For the professional and volunteer working with young urban males it is critical that they obtain and maintain an intrinsic knowledge of street culture and the dynamics associated with the requirements of being "male" in the urban street culture eco-system.

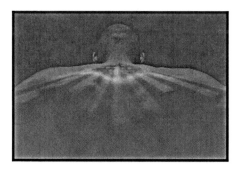

Seven

"What's a good girl?"
Londa, age 12

Growing Up Urban and Female

Effecting change...

"All of us must listen and respond to the cries for help and despair coming from the [female] children and youths in our neighborhoods, on our street corners, in our schools, and in our families. We must work together to change these young [urban] women's vision for the future. We must stop the proliferation of guns. We must implement a range of violence prevention strategies including anti-violence curricula and such positive alternatives as after school service, recreation, tutoring, and mentoring opportunities. And we must confront our cultural obsession with violence hawked in the media, television, movies, and advertisements. Finally, we must examine the deepest values of our culture which measures success by things—things we kill for—rather than by community strength and mutual support. We will all pay now and later if we continue to ignore our youth's fight for survival."

Source: Marian Wright Edelman: In Girl's, gangs, women, and drugs
(C. S. Taylor, 1993) (p. 1)

Urban youth are often faced with negative influences that engulf their everyday existence. It is challenging to grow up as a young woman in an environment where violence is executed upon her in multifaceted dimensions. Violence is often thought of as physical harm. This definition is very narrow. Violence is not only domestic, mental, and physical abuse; it is the high poverty rate that the urban population suffers; the rampant onslaught of HIV/AIDS in the African American community; daily oppression instituted through racism, sexism and classism; poor education; and the normalization of behavior from stereotypes that define many young women as loose and immoral in popular music and media.

Growing up in an urban environment as a young woman is very complex. According to researchers urban communities have higher poverty rates, crime and delinquency, and adolescent females have a higher likely hood of becoming pregnant and being a single mother. The challenges of an urban community that has little resources for its young women in today's anything goes society are specifically challenging during adolescence. Their diverse experiences embody direct links to their self-esteem, perception, health issues, and possible alcohol and drug experimentation.

It must be noted that urban issues and conditions are not exclusive to the African American community but there is a disproportionate number of African Americans living in poor urban communities throughout the United States. With this fact in mind it is pointed out that young women of all ethnic origins are subject to the same conditions and problems in urban America. In many instances the issue is one of class and poverty rather than one ethnicity.

Eight

"I know that I can make it, I'm hard."
Maxi, age 19

*"I don't know nothing about street life, I'm about
being happy & smart."*
Malinda, age 16

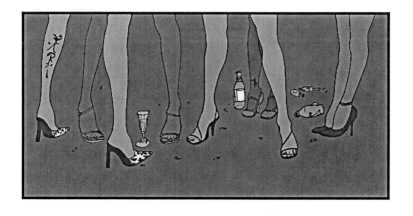

Perception of the Urban Girl

Answering the question "Who am I?" is a complicated matter. Feeling good about yourself is intertwined with race, ethnicity, class, and gender (Erkut, Fields, Sing, & Marx, 1996). Self esteem, body image and identity are linked and can be influenced by life experiences, society, and cultural background during pre-adolescent and adolescent developing years (Erkut et al., 1996; Talking, 2003).

The recent trend in musical lyrics where young women are being called, "bitch, ho, and tip drill" are alarming to say the least. As stated by West in January's Essence, "My fear is that girls don't even see their own victimization anymore. They say, 'I'm a bitch, I'm a ho, I'm a tip drill.' As porn moves more into the mainstream, it only normalizes the behavior and how we deal with sexual assault and violence (Byrd & Solomon, 2005)."

The media portrays urban girls through a very narrowly focused lens. When we see them on magazine covers and in music videos they are skimpily dressed with their bare breasts and butts often seen (Editors, 2005). Russell Simmons, cofounder of Def Jam Records and chairman of Hip-hop Summit Action Network states, "There is no question that the sexism in hip-hop videos is a reflection of how sexist men are in the world today (Byrd & Solomon, 2005)."

Here are a number of questions taken from the "Body Image Inventory" constructed by the Sexuality Information and Education Council of the United States for self analysis to gain awareness of positive or negative feelings or images a young woman may have of herself (Talking, 2003):

-What's the first positive message you remember receiving about your body? Negative message? How old were you? How have these messages impacted you?

-What messages do you wish you received about body image and self- esteem as you were growing up?

-What do you like best about your body? What about your body, if anything, do you compare to an "ideal" that the media portrays? Do you find yourself trying to alter your body to meet this ideal? If so, how?

When assessing the answers regarding body image it should be taken into consideration that desiring to look, act and/or dress like the depicted images of young women in the media and videos doesn't necessarily indicate low self-esteem. In fact, researchers have noted that despite racism and prejudice many African-American girls level of self-esteem doesn't drop during adolescence (Frankel, 2003).

Weaving ethnicity, gender, sexuality, and class during adolescence to form a sense of identity, is considered the primary developmental task by Erickson (Erickson, 1968, as cited in (Shorter-Gooden & Washington, 1996) in this stage of life. According to Shorter-Gooden & Washington (1996) identity is a self-definition of a person's goals, values and beliefs. Stevens (1997) found that identity formation for adolescent African-American females to be multidimensional and complex. She suggests that identity is processed from synthesizing the following three social experiences:

-Mainstream society (European American world view).

-A devalued societal status (affected by the status convergence of gender and race).

-Cultural reference group (Afro-American world view).

Nine

"I'm a gangster; don't even think I'm some soft girlie."
Indigo, age 25

Urban Girls,
Crime & Delinquency

 Urban communities are experiencing an influx of African American adolescent females into the juvenile justice system. Wayne County, which includes the City of Detroit and is the state's most urban county, is wrestling with growing numbers of female youth in juvenile detention and placement (Skillman Center for Children, 2002). Juvenile crime rates have dropped 23% since 1995, and yet the arrest rate for girls is increasing at a rapid pace (Children's Defense Fund, 2001). The National Council on Crime and Delinquency (NCCD) reported that approximately two-thirds of the girls in the juvenile justice system are mostly African American and Hispanic (Acoca, 1999).

Girls are increasingly becoming more violent. The insurgence of violence and delinquency by girls has become a national phenomenon. In addition, the crime rate for girls has increased (Snyder & Sickmund, 1999). Times have changed and some teen-age girls no longer strive to be yesterday's definition of a lady; they are embracing the persona of a thug. Taylor (1993) noted in his research that young women in Detroit were not only members of gangs, but some had their own crews.

When girls in the study were asked if they were afraid of the violence in the streets, the following summation represents the attitude of several respondents: Violence is an everyday occurrence and a female can't be soft, she has to be hard or fellas in the hood will run her over. Others contend that they don't condone violence and that fighting and shooting in their neighborhood happened all the time.

In their research, Campbell (1984), Deschenes and Esbensen (1999), and Chesney-Lind (1999) also recognized the existence of female gangs and their tendency to be violent. Moreover, Deschenes and Esbensen (1999) contend that gang girls are more violent than non-gang boys.

Several girls and women were featured as a recent example of violence among girls in *The Detroit News*, when a twelve year-old girl was brutally attacked at a birthday party. She was kissed on the cheek by the birthday girl's boyfriend as a dare from the other kids at the party. The birthday girl's mother not only instructed her daughter to assault the victim; she was also a participant in the fight (Hall, 2004). Over ten years ago, Taylor (1993) found that inner-city girls in his study were absorbed in violence. Specifically, girls were carrying weapons (e.g., guns) and getting into violent fights.

The chaos and disharmony experienced in urban America has lead to the hopelessness young women sense in their environment. The outward display of violence by girls is a manifestation of society's unwillingness to embrace them.

Ten

"I hate guns, I hate violence, I just want to live like anybody else."
Samantha, age 20

The Impact of Violence on Young Urban Females

 Young women are impacted by violence in places such as the home, school, neighborhood, community, or workplace. It was once thought that children witnessing violent situations while young would forget or be too young to comprehend the incident. Research now shows that young children can remember violent acts in vivid detail (Wilson, 2000). The National Center for Injury Prevention and Control (NCIPC), which is a division of the Centers for Disease Control (CDC), compiled several fact sheets related to violence.

The Youth Violence Fact Sheet details several occurrences and consequences for youth nationally. Although all of the facts are pertinent to urban communities, the following two facts were of particular importance (Control, 2004):

1) Homicide is the second leading cause of death among young people ages 10 to 24 overall. In this age group, it is the leading cause of death for African-Americans, the second leading cause of death for Hispanics, and the third leading cause of death for American Indians, Alaskan Natives, and Asian Pacific Islanders.

2) A nationwide survey found female students (12%) more likely than male students (6%) to have been forced to have sexual intercourse.

Note that from the Intimate Partner Violence (IPV) Fact Sheet these individual risk factors were identified as contributors to women (young women) being vulnerable to violent acts:

- Young age

- Low self-esteem

- Low income

- Low academic achievement

- Involvement in aggressive or delinquent behavior as a youth

- Alcohol use

- Drug use

-Witnessing or experiencing violence as a child

- Lack of social networks and social isolation

- Unemployment

Eleven

"Some fellas think being female means you're soft, stupid or something."
Ella, age 14

"Me, no-way-No babies!"
Sarise, age 16

Sexuality and the Young Urban Female

Understanding the context in which young urban women view their adolescent sexuality is important. The complexity of issues centered on sexual development has taken a back seat to a single issue, "teen pregnancy." According to Tolman (Tolman, 1996), urban girls have been stereotyped as immoral, unemployed, not successful in school, sexually promiscuous, unable to delay gratification, out of control, and lacking family values.

From a societal point of view, Tolman states, "The Urban Girl is [seen as] bad and not normal: she is female adolescent sexuality. So imagined and constructed, she bears the brunt of society's collective anxiety in altered, punitive forms. She is the dumping ground for the strongest and most suppressed fears and desires regarding sexuality." In her study she gave urban and suburban girls a voice. Tolman found that girls struggle with their sexual desire as they negotiate through adolescent development.

To grasp a clearer understanding of how girls integrate sexuality into their identity it is suggested that sexuality should be researched independent of pregnancy and deviance (Tolman, 1996). A list of questions was formulated by Tolman (1996) that address issues of sexuality for all girls:

1) When girls engage in sexual encounters, are they experiencing pleasure?

2) Do they know what they want or desire sexually?

3) In what contexts can they act on their own feelings?

4) Are there differences in psychological vitality between girls with positive sexual self-concepts and those without?

Understanding the Obstacles Facing the Young Urban Female

Poverty stricken neighborhoods, inadequate education, teen pregnancy, domestic violence and, drug and alcohol distribution and usage are some of the obstacles that challenge the healthy social development of young urban females. According to Jargowsky (Jargowsky, 1997), poor neighborhoods have more single-female headed households of people of color and less educated adults.

Similarly, Taylor, Tucker, Chatters, and Jayakody (R. J. Taylor, Tucker, Chatters, & Jayakody, 1997) have found that one of several factors influencing the high level of poverty among African American children is higher rates of female-headed households among African Americans. In addition, they contend that childhood poverty is strongly linked to a child's living arrangements and that living in poverty places children at risk for serious health problems, low educational achievement, and minimal labor market participation.

In addition, overcoming the heavy influence of street culture which is dominant in video games, clothes, language and, even the cars driven by today's youth is also a major obstacle. Grand Theft Auto: San Andreas is a popular video game that takes place in an urban community plagued with poverty, gangs, drugs, and corrupt police officers. This medium shows a community living with daily violence. Throughout the game women of color are referred to as a "bitch" and/or "ho" and they are portrayed in provocative clothing with a hard core demeanor using profane language (Houser, Pooh, & Worrall, 2004).

Constant exposure to these derogatory images and vernacular while playing the game may be a factor in desensitizing the public to violence and misogynistic attitudes directed toward urban women of color.

Twelve

"I got to have my own ride, that is freedom."
Sondrese, age 20

Pimp My Ride

This television show takes the old and dilapidated vehicle of an urban youth and turns it into state of the art transportation. This is just one example of immediate gratification that Generation X feels they are entitled to. "Youth [females] are not making the connection that it takes hard work, education, and time to acquire the money it takes to own a pimped out ride or other material possessions. Then again, they may recognize the concept, but do not understand the value, and with limited opportunities some girls choose from two of the most prevalent choices for young women which are found in legal or illegal avenues illegal (e.g., prostitution, robbery, drug sales,), and legal, e.g., in the fast growing rap industry (e.g., dancing in videos, stripping) (Smith-Minifee, 2004)."

Young girls want to wear the clothes and jewelry, and have the boyfriend that they see in videos or hear in today's songs (Smith-Minifee, 2004). It is a challenge to help them distinguish between what is entertainment and what is a choice with positive outcomes. Gaining an understanding of how negative choices and images impact their future well-being is needed in gender specific programming.

Resources in the form of good education, job opportunities, positive role models, and community programs implementing positive youth development are needed to foster skills for young women to become healthy and productive citizens.

The Future and the Young Urban Female

Urban girls are in need of gender specific programs in their immediate communities that foster positive youth development. As poor and young women of color grow up in urban communities their adolescent development is processed through exposure to complex and multi-faceted circumstances.

Forty-five years ago a poem was written about the urban environment and street culture. It is simple and to the point. Consider its meaning and the message is one that can be applied to today's youth as well.

We Real Cool, a poem
By
Gwendolyn Brooks

We real cool. We
Left school. We
Lurk late. We
Strike straight. We
Sing sin. We
Thin gin. We
Jazz June. We
Die soon.

Source: Gwendolyn Brooks: In The Bean Eaters (Brooks, 1960)

Thirteen

"You got to be careful, got to take care of yourself."
Alese, age 18

"I don't smoke, drink and I don't sex, these are scary times - I wanna live..."
Sheri, age 28

Health Issues Affecting African American Women/Community

Young people think that they are invincible. Without the proper education, be it from parents, school, peers, or the community, they are vulnerable to life threatening diseases. Obesity and HIV/AIDS are two health crises that the urban community needs to educationally arm themselves against. Consider these facts in reference to Obesity and African American women:

• According to the American Heart Association 2003 Heart Disease and Stroke Statistical Update, African American women are significantly more likely than white women, Mexican American women or Hispanic women to be overweight (body mass index [BMI] of 25 to 29.9) or obese (BMI of 30 or greater). Whereas about three out of every 10 African American men, white men or white women are obese, almost five out of 10 African American women are obese.

• Compared to whites, African American women have almost double the risk of a first-ever stroke.

• The American Obesity Association reported that, in comparison with other Americans,

African American women tend to have greater body fat and more weight-related complications, such as diabetes and high blood pressure.

• Research has shown an association between insulin resistance and dietary deficiency of some minerals. For example, low levels of magnesium may correlate to an increased risk of high blood pressure and diabetes. Studies find a higher incidence of magnesium deficiency among African-Americans, as compared to other ethnic groups. It is difficult, however, to directly measure magnesium levels, since only trace amounts are normally present in blood. Individuals with high blood pressure and/or diabetes may wish to discuss with their physician the Dash diet, which is high in magnesium, potassium and calcium – and low in sodium. The Dash diet, and other well tested dietary approaches have been proven to lower blood pressure in African Americans, and are promoted by the International Society of Hypertension in Blacks and by the Association of Black Cardiologists.

• Although the traditional African American high-calorie diet developed as a way to sustain people whose primary job involved heavy physical labor, it now provides too many daily calories for the average person leading a sedentary lifestyle. The traditional diet is high in saturated fat, calories and protein. It includes pork, chicken and beef, with vegetables and rice/potatoes seasoned with the grease of these meats. The typical African American diet appears to be unhealthy all over the United States – more so in Southern states, according to some studies. The new additions to the traditional African American diet are fast food: burgers, hot dogs, pizza and French fries (cooked in oil full of trans fatty acids).

- According to the American Obesity Association, overweight affects African American women (and men), regardless of socioeconomic status.

- Statistically, African American women tend to have more financial challenges than white women, so they are less likely to spend money on joining a gym or a national weight loss center. Gyms, health clubs and other weight-loss facilities are also less common in African American communities than other neighborhoods.

- Some believe that the African American culture tends to value heavier women as healthy and attractive, despite the fact that extra pounds put extra stress on the heart. Other cultural issues (e.g., choice in hairstyle) may make it difficult for African American women to exercise.

• African American women appear to have a slower metabolism than white women, meaning they burn fewer calories at rest.

• African American women appear to be less physically active than other women. They also report engaging in less exercise as they get older, according to the American Obesity Association.

Source: Heart Center Online: For Cardiologists & Their Patients (Perry-Botinger, 2004)

Did you know that the urban community is at risk of loosing future generations from the spread of HIV/ AIDS? No, there is recent data for people of color that documents this epidemic. Facts to consider about HIV/AIDS and women of color from the United States Department of Human Services, Office of the Surgeon General:

• Of the estimated 886, 575 Americans that have been diagnosed since the beginning of the epidemic through 2002, 159,271 of those occurred in adult and adolescent females.

Black and Hispanic women account for roughly 78 percent of those cases, and Asian/ Pacific Islander and American Indian/Alaska Native women comprise nearly 1 percent of those cases.

- The proportion of Aids diagnoses among women, especially among women of color, has increased since the beginning of the epidemic. Women represent 26 percent of new AIDS diagnoses in 2002, compared to only 11 percent of new AIDS cases reported in 1990.

- Black and Hispanic women accounted for 80 percent of all women estimated to be living with AIDS, with Black women making up 59 percent of the total alone.

- Women across racial/ethnic groups most commonly report heterosexual contact or injection drug use as their primary modes of exposure to HIV.

- HIV/AIDS was the leading cause of death among African American women ages 25-34 in 2001. HIV/AIDS was also the fourth leading cause of death for Hispanic women ages 35-44.

• An estimated 886, 575 Americans have been diagnosed with AIDS from the beginning of the epidemic through 2002. Of the 42,136 estimated new diagnoses in 2002, 74 percent were male and 26 percent were female. Less than 1 percent were children under 13.

• African Americans account for 39 percent of total estimated AIDS diagnoses through 2002, though they make up only 12.7 percent of the population. They also represent an estimated 54 percent of persons newly diagnosed with HIV in 200s.

• Hispanics account for 18 percent of total estimated AIDS diagnoses through 2002, though they make up only 13.4 percent of the population.

• The number of Asian/Pacific Islanders and American Indian/Alaska Natives living with AIDS continues to rise, with an approximately 10 percent increase each year over the past 5 years.

Source: United States Department of Human Services (HIV/ AIDS and minority women, 2004)

As an Urban community, Detroit has an alarming profile of the epidemic, HIV/AIDS. How does Detroit compare with near by counties?

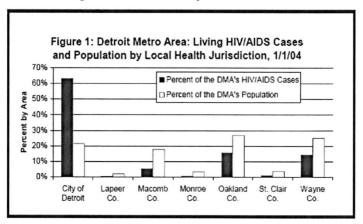

Figure 1: Detroit Metro Area: Living HIV/AIDS Cases and Population by Local Health Jurisdiction, 1/1/04

Source: 2004 Profile of HIV/AIDS: The Detroit Metro Area (2004)

The 2004 Profile of HIV/AIDS: The Detroit Metro Area offers this Summary of Epidemic for The Detroit Area:

How many cases?

The Michigan Department of Community Health (MDCH) estimates that there are 10,500 people living with HIV? AIDS in the Detroit Metro Area, of which 7,337 were reported as of January 1, 2004. For this profile, the Detroit Metro Area is the Detroit Metropolitan Statistical Area as defined by the US Census. It contains the counties of Lapeer, Oakland, Macomb, Monroe,

121

St. Clair, and Wayne, including the city of Detroit. The incidence of HIV (the number of new HIV infections) was roughly level at around 500 new cases each year between 1998 and 2002. The number of AIDS deaths annually in the Detroit Metro Area has remained roughly level at about 210 deaths each year between 1998 and 2002. However, the prevalence of HIV disease (all persons living with HIV infection or AIDS, whether diagnosed recently or years ago) is increasing because new cases are still being diagnosed and infected persons are living longer.

How are the cases geographically distributed?

HIV disease is distributed disproportionately in Michigan. The Detroit Metro Area has more cases (7,337 of the 11,527 cases reported in Michigan) when compared with the number of people who live there. Within the Detroit Metro Area, the City of Detroit has a higher proportion of cases than expected based on the percent of the population that lives there. Figure 1 displays the distribution of reported cases by local health jurisdictions within the Detroit Metro Area. Sixty-three percent of the reported cases within this area were among residents of Detroit.

• The 83 counties of Michigan are divided into 45 local health departments (LHDs). In the less populated areas of the state LHDs may contain more than one county, however most contain a single county. All LHDs have been labeled as either being in a high or low HIV prevalence area (please refer to Figure 2, page 3-6 of the Statewide profile for methodology used [in the original report]). Within the Detroit Metro Area, the City of Detroit and Oakland and Wayne counties are considered to be LHDs in high prevalence areas (93 percent of cases in the Detroit Metro Area), while Lapeer, Macomb, Monroe and St. Clair counties are considered to be LHDs in low prevalence areas.

Source: 2004 Profile of HIV/AIDS: The Detroit Metro Area (2004)

These health crises are detrimental to the urban community. Educating the population is a must. The alarm is not sounding loud enough about these diseases. Young urban women are in serious trouble if they don't learn to protect themselves.

Fourteen

"RESEARCH? Folks that ask too much about your business."
Mary, age 24

Methods, Techniques & Tools

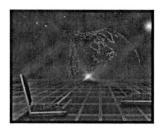

The modern child/youth development professional and volunteer has at his/her disposal a wealth of knowledge and information to assist in achieving his/her personal goals and/or objectives and/or those of their organization or agency. One research organization, the Critical Analysis Group, utilizes several tools developed over the past thirty years of researching and analyzing children, youth and families throughout the United States, Europe, Africa and parts of South America.

The most effective tools have been found to be those that provide the researcher, worker, etc., with a solid understanding of the community they work in, an easy and effective method to track those forces that influence and impact the community and a reliable tool to track and chart outcomes and results. It is noted that the research of CAG does not support any "cookie cutter" methodology whereby it is considered that one person or body knows best what applies to all communities, groups, organizations, families, etc.

Many community groups, agencies and organizations already have very effective methods and methodologies in place for achieving their goals and objectives. The following tools and concepts are supplied for consideration and/or use as deemed appropriate based on individual and/or organizational needs.

Fifteen

"You cant really say much if you don't know much about round here."
Byron Willson, age 86

The Eco-Scan

The Eco-Scan is a research method used to review collected data to better understand the environment. Particularly useful in understanding issues and the forces at work in urban communities, this process utilizes tools for the critical analysis of the connectivity between all elements of the community. Data track items used in the CAG (Critical Analysis Group) Eco-Scan include but are not limited to the following:

- Number of abandoned homes & properties in a neighborhood.

- Lighting conditions in a neighborhood.

- Number of liquor stores and bars in a neighborhood.

- Number of local recreational facilities in a neighborhood/(conditions of facilities).

- Evidence of drug dealing (sale & purchase) activity in a neighborhood (detail regarding locations, frequency, etc).

- Condition of properties (buildings & lots) in a neighborhood.

- Number of active churches in a neighborhood.

- Number of schools in a neighborhood.

- Crime statistics of neighborhood.

- Number of local businesses in a neighborhood.

- Success/failure rate of middle and high schools in a neighborhood (graduation/drop-out rate).

- Size of police force in a neighborhood (number of law enforcement officers assigned to local precincts).

- Evidence of prostitution in a neighborhood.

- Availability of grocery stores, drug stores, hardware stores, etc.

- Availability of easily assessable health care professionals.

- Does a neighborhood have an active block club?

- Number of financial institutions in a neighborhood.

- Availability and ease of access to public transportation.

The Eco-Scan is an adjustable tool that can provide valuable insight into the assets and liabilities of a neighborhood/community.

Designed to be flexible the Eco-Scan not only provides data for researchers it can also be utilized to assist those working in a community to better connect with other agencies and organizations dedicated to the improvement of the community. If desired and/or required the Eco-Scan can be utilized as a longitudinal research tool as it allows for study of the evolution of a neighborhood/community over a definite or indefinite time-line.

Sixteen

"You gotta git in where you fit in."
Too Short

The Trojan Horse

The Trojan Horse is a conceptual intervention model based on the concept of infiltration by stealth. Those familiar with the story of Helen of Troy will remember that the Greeks breached the impenetrable walls of the city of Troy by hiding inside a large horse presented as a gift to the mighty Trojans. Once the city of Troy was asleep, the Greeks emerged from inside the Trojan Horse, opened the gates for their waiting warriors and defeated the Trojans.

Today a growing culture of ignorance and violence prevails in our urban communities. Those that continue to rely on traditional means and methods are finding themselves facing a virtual army of proponents, advocates and practitioners of this new "street culture". To preach traditional doctrine to the hordes of devotee's to this prevalent culture is not only usually a waste of time it is self-defeating and can be potentially dangerous.

The Trojan Horse approach utilizes a theory that does not embrace the ideologies associated with the negative aspects of street culture but rather relies on understanding the signs, symbols, theories and language of the culture. In understanding those components that comprise this new and ever evolving culture one can help to mold the culture by utilizing its own positive aspects and attributes.

One of the most damaging techniques frequently utilized by adults (professionals, volunteers and others that interact with children and youth) is the "downing" of "hip-hop" and other youth oriented music and culture. While it is noted that many adults do not approve of or appreciate "hip-hop" and other forms of youth genre music it is important to note that dismissing these forms of music and their associated cultures only helps to widen the gap between the adult and the young person they are trying to reach.

The Trojan Horse approach to dealing with "hip-hop" (note that this approach can be used with any ideology, fad or culture) provides the adult working with young people the ability to look past those negative aspects of the culture to why and how it motivates, stimulates or otherwise affects the young person.

If dialogue can be established regarding the numerous and varied aspects of the culture then progress can be made toward the positive development of the young person and ultimately the community.

The Trojan Horse approach does not suggest that a person must change his or her views, values, beliefs or philosophy. To the contrary this approach relies on the ability of people to effectively communicate by putting aside personal differences in the effort to better understand the position of another for the betterment of oneself and the larger society.

The Trojan Horse approach is designed to infiltrate a state of thinking and thereby stimulate positive, progressive thinking ultimately resulting in the destruction of the growing appreciation for ignorance and violence. It is noted that this theory is a process and not a "quick fix", it has taken years for this current culture to take root and spread, it will not reverse overnight. The question arises as to how to effectively apply the Trojan Horse approach.

As indicated there is no "quick fix" to addressing modern issues pertaining to dealing with urban youth. Dialogue is key to success, but perhaps more importantly is the demonstration of respect for those things that young people feel are important.

It can be difficult for an adult to accept ideas, concepts and activities they feel are inappropriate, and while they may be correct they will find themselves totally ineffective if they reveal their misgivings to the very young people that they are trying to positively affect.

One primary weapon that can be used to deliver fatal blows to ignorance and abhorrent behavior is factual information and revealing proof of the irreversible and damaging effects of certain behaviors. Young people frequently believe that adults know little if anything about pop culture, youth culture and street culture, typically they are correct. Youth culture relies on a continually morphing system of symbols, words, concepts, ideas, idols, etc. This complex array represents a world that provides its denizens power and control exclusive of the larger society.

Adult culture typically too deeply rooted in its own system of values, beliefs and ideas based in part on laws, rules and regulations but also on a system of shared values that are in part inherited, are generally oblivious to knowledge and information relative to youth culture. The adult professional or volunteer that seeks to penetrate youth culture and positively influence young people will find it beneficial to stay abreast of news and information as it relates to youth culture and street culture. Knowing the latest video games, what the latest rumors are regarding urban myth and street tales demonstrates to the young person that the things that matter to them are important to this person that claims to be concerned with their best interest.

The weapon of factual information can be utilized to dispel misinformation, provide motivation and repudiate dangerous myths. In situations where young people believe that some of their famous sports and music idols achieved their success "overnight" having accurate information regarding the celebrity can give rise to beneficial and meaningful dialogue.

A recent focus group involving approximately 30 urban teens demonstrates how this approach can be applied: During discussion several members of the group discussed their plans to become superstar rappers and therefore they had no interest in completing school or working. One of the facilitators asked what the general consensus was regarding this approach to a career path.

Almost unanimously the group advised that this was in fact a realistic approach to establishing a viable career whereby they could basically party, do very little work and make a substantial income in a very short period of time. As discussion regarding this method of "blowing up" continued the group became more excited and animated as they laid out their grandiose plans for success.

The facilitator listened and allowed the animated conversation to continue for several minutes and then acknowledged that such a lifestyle and career did indeed sound intriguing. He then asked how familiar the group was with the rap superstar Jay-Z otherwise known as Shawn Carter. The group quieted, obviously a little caught off guard that the facilitator (an adult) knew something about Jay-

Z. Seizing the moment the facilitator engaged the group in conversation about this famous rapper and his organization.

Having done his homework the facilitator knew the history of Mr. Carter and his organization, the fact that Jay-Z was not an overnight success and in fact had worked very diligently in the entertainment industry for many years prior to achieving any modicum of success at all. He further went on to reveal that many of the key members of his Rocafella organization were college graduates. Discussion regarding the music of Mr. Carter provided dialogue that was promising as it sparked debates about the many different positive and negative aspects of street culture.

Ultimately when the session ended the facilitator seemed to have gained a newfound respect from the young people in the focus group. Many of the members of the group agreed that perhaps it was best that they considered a more business based entrepreneurial approach to achieving their dreams of stardom.

This is just one method of applying the Trojan Horse approach to addressing urban youth culture but it can be a very effective method. It is not suggested that the professional or volunteer attempt to change their own preferences or opinions regarding urban youth culture but rather that they acknowledge the importance of understanding it and being knowledgeable about those things that matter to urban youth.

When engaging young people about things applicable to their culture the opportunity will frequently arise to make a positive change in the life of a young person. Having facts pertaining to myths and misconceptions often provides the ability to correct those misconceptions and dispel many of the myths. This method is far more beneficial than attempting to stand on what one believes is a superior position based on their own background, morality, education or other beliefs, ideas and concepts.

Seventeen

"It is best to just chill, too many folks got serious issues."
Zani, age 14

The Umpire Theory

Umpires and game officials are in, most cases, in situations that will make them unpopular. The decisions they make will invariably displease some fans, spectators, coaches, and players. To be successful in this role an umpire must possess a variety of skills and attributes. First, the umpire must be knowledgeable about the rules of the game, additionally, he/she must be able to effectively communicate, handle difficult and potentially volatile situations, make decisions with confidence (some of which will be unpopular), be able to accept and handle criticism, and maintain strong self concepts including, self-worth, self-esteem, and confidence. Such skills are critical for umpires but also represent a valuable set of important skills for all individuals and are particularly important for developing children and youth as they grow and learn.

Developing a program that allows children and young people to serve in "umpire/referee" roles would provide "real world" practice using the skills mentioned earlier in addition to facilitating the development of leadership skills. One of the most beneficial aspects of implementing such a concept is that sports programs in need of officiating are already in existence. There are competitive sports leagues and intramural programs throughout communities that require the utilization of umpires and referee's.

One of the challenges faced by many communities is how to provide officials for child and youth games. In an age of increasing limitations of resources many programs would benefit from having qualified youth game officials. Sporting event officials are typically paid, but it can be a challenge to find adults with the time to dedicate to officiating child and youth games. An established youth umpire/referee corps would serve as both a youth development program and youth employment program. There is extraordinary potential for such a dual prong program in the urban community.

The basics of the program include training and real world experience coupled with the opportunity for the young participant to demonstrate and practice important life skills in game environments and situations. Youth umpires/referee's would be trained in conflict resolution, communication, and other components of the "umpire" skill set. Learning the rules of the games will enhance reading, interpretation, and ultimately critical thinking skills that will be put into practice during games or team practices. The importance of this concept is that it takes theories and concepts and applies them to real world contexts for young people. The concepts of self-discipline and self-control are actively practiced while officiating games. Other continuing skill practice opportunities include but are not limited to leadership, responsibility, making unpopular decisions, fairness, decision-making, and others.

Winning While Losing

The doctrine of "winning while losing" is a unique concept that was presented during an exchange of ideas regarding working to positively affect our youth and children. Mr. Randy McNeil of the YSRC revealed some of his ideas and methods for working with children, youth and adults in the community. During the discussion Mr. McNeil told of an experience where some men were drinking and using profanity at a youth sporting event he was involved in.

Mr. McNeil engaged the men and appealed to their (not very obvious) sense of decency to demonstrate more appropriate behavior in light of the event and the fact that there were women and children in the area. One of the men reportedly became belligerent and even more vulgar as he informed Mr. McNeil that he would do as he pleased.

Recognizing that the situation could potentially escalate into a hostile and dangerous incident Mr.

McNeil reportedly smiled at the gentleman and his friends and thanked them for their support before walking away. As he walked away he overheard the other men in the group chastising the obstinate, belligerent man for his behavior. Reportedly the man grumbled and cursed a bit before reluctantly agreeing that perhaps he was wrong and the entire group of men changed their behavior so that it was more suitable to the event.

Mr. McNeil calls this technique "winning while losing" and indeed it is a method that can frequently be used when facing adversity. On the surface it might have appeared that Mr. McNeil had not only placed himself in danger by approaching these men but that he had exacerbated the situation and lost face in the process. To the contrary, by appealing to the decency of the group Mr. McNeil achieved his objective.

By not engaging in a demonstration of machismo or bravado and relying instead on common sense and a sense of decency he managed to cause the other men in the group to correct the error of the behaviors being demonstrated. While it might have appeared to the casual observer that Mr. McNeil lost to the more aggressive, larger force he faced he in fact won because his goal was met.

In dealing with many situations while working with people in any community the ability to appeal to their sense of decency or propriety will frequently provide the ability to win while it might appear that one is losing.

This is a doctrine that may provide benefit time and again to the professional or volunteer working in the urban community. It must be remembered that it requires a cool head and strong sense of purpose to not demonstrate fear nor frustration or anger in the face of adversity...winning while losing provides a "win, win" for everyone when applied properly.

Eighteen

"My grandmother says to stay in control, let 'em act stupid. Better to let it go, live another day."
Shawn, age 16

Music as a Tool
The Rap on Urban Youth Music

"I see hip-hop communication as a continuation of the old school: Lester Young and Count Basie and everyone in the subculture were using the words "homeboy" and "rap" back in the forties. Bebop was all about not just instrumentation but also scat, vocalese, and attitude. Hip-hop can sometimes come out at the raw end of the spectrum, and some of it has been polluted by the hustle-the big cars and the obsession with the Benjamins and worst of all by the violence of brothers killing brothers, most of it perpetuated not by rappers but by the gangs who've appropriated the music in the name of "keeping it real". Our country's greatest cultural contributions, whether you're talking about jazz and gospel, an Irish jig or black tap dancing, the Broadway musical, barbershop, doo-wop, bebop, or rhythm and blues, reflect our gumbo nature. Now even the most hard-core rap is playing in shopping malls in Dallas not to mention Estonia, Paris, and Tokyo, and on the African continent itself."

Source: Quincy Jones: In Q The Autobiography of Quincy Jones (Q. Jones, 2001) (p. 285)

Quincy Jones is recognized throughout the world as one of the most respected and prolific composers, arrangers, musicians, writers and producers of modern times. In his autobiography he dedicates an entire chapter to hip-hop. As evidenced in his quote many of the terms now associated with hip-hop have their roots in urban culture dating back to more than a half a century ago. For most urban youth hip-hop is their music, it is a serious part of life for many young people in urban communities throughout not only America but the world.

Hip-hop is in the year 2005 what rock and roll was to many young people in 1965. Whether you like it or not, hip-hop is the voice of a generation and contrary to the belief of some, it is not relegated strictly to urban communities. For many urban youth hip-hop is their voice, it represents the struggles and challenges they feel that they face daily in their lives. Some hip-hop notables (particularly rappers) have achieved iconic status in youth culture.

The adult that dismisses or diminishes the importance of a hip-hop icon will likely find themselves shut out by the young people that they are attempting to interact with.

For the professional or volunteer working with urban youth it is important to understand the music and symbols that are so very important to them.

The ability to demonstrate some knowledge of their music oftentimes will provide the opportunity to establish dialogue that might not otherwise exist. It is important to note that gaining an understanding of hip-hop culture also provides the ability to dispel misconceptions that many young people have regarding facts related to the culture.

Not all urban youngsters are engaged in hip-hop music or culture but it is the dominant musical genre and culture in most modern urban communities. For the person working with children and young people it is critically important to gain some knowledge of the dominant culture, its music and symbols and to be aware that such cultures are in a continual state of flux and subsequently constantly changing.

Certain aspects of hip-hop culture may remain relatively stable while other aspects may seem to change almost weekly. An example of this is the type or style of rap. Some years ago rappers like M.C. Hammer were popular (though briefly and that may be debated by some hard-core hip-hop aficionado's) in the hip-hop world of the day.

Today the mere mention of M.C. Hammer will evoke blank stares, riotous laughter and/ or grunts of disgust from youth immersed in modern hip-hop culture. If an adult is going to use certain aspects of youth culture as a tool it is wise to really be familiar with the culture and not attempt to as the young people say "front". The world of hip-hop is vast and diverse; there are those that refuse to acknowledge as legitimate any aspect of the culture that does not belong to the "gangsta" philosophy and style of rap. Others embrace a wider range of the music and culture which may include gospel or religious rap, Afro-centric positive rap, etc.

Familiarity with the type of hip-hop (or other musical genre or culture) a young person or groups of young people are embracing can provide insights into ideologies or concepts that they might be embracing. This is not to suggest that a young person or group might be prone to violent behavior because they listen to or favor a particular style or type of hip-hop. Many young people understand that any form of music, video, movie, etc is simply entertainment. Unfortunately far too often the lines do become blurred for young people in urban communities and life imitates art with disastrous results.

When establishing dialogue using hip-hop as a tool it might be important to discuss the image of a particular hip-hop star, the type of music they make, the lifestyles they portray, etc. Once dialogue is established then reality can often be separated from fiction, concepts can be discussed and the potential is created to positively impact the young person(s) involved in the dialogue. It cannot be stressed enough just how important it is to never dismiss, ridicule or diminish the importance of the prevalent popular youth culture whether it is hip-hop, grunge or some other genre that has yet to emerge.

Nineteen

"That's all we got, our music."
F-U, age 19 (Rapper)

Rules of Engagement

Adults working with children and youth must at all times remain professional and observe rules that will ensure the avoidance of any perception of impropriety or illegality. While some of the rules set out herein are purely common sense and good ideas, others are based on the need to as much as possible eliminate any potential for criminal charges, civil lawsuits, violent episodes and other problems that can and do arise when a breakdown in proper child/adult relationship protocols occur.

This list of rules is not conclusive as it is recognized that all organizations and many situations may have particular issues that require special rules to address special circumstances and/or situations. Perhaps the best "rule" to always remember is; if an appearance of inappropriateness might be evident, the activity or behavior should be avoided.

On the next page are the top ten rules of engagement for interacting with children and youth.

The Top Ten Rules of Engagement

1. Do not engage in physical displays of affection beyond what is considered appropriate; appropriate displays of care and affection are typically limited to a brief hug or gentle pat on the upper back.

2. Do not have closed door meetings with a child unless another authorized adult is present in the room.

3. Do not loan or give money to children or their families.

4. Do not authorize children or young people to engage in any activities that are not specifically identified on parent/guardian authorization forms.

5. Do not engage in gossip with children and young people.

6. Do not use profanity in front of children and young people.

7. Refrain from discussions about sex unless specific guidelines are established and approved of by your governing or authorizing agency. When topics related to sex are discussed with young adults it is imperative that such discussions are held in the proper context and with parent or guardian knowledge and approval.

8. Do not engage in physical contact with children and young people beyond what is necessary to provide training and instruction; some examples include but are not limited to coaches that are required to touch a child to demonstrate proper technique, trainers that assist a young person with proper body positioning, etc.

9. Do not get personally involved in the lives of parents, guardians and other influential adults in the lives of children and young people.

10. Do not establish situations where communications are encouraged outside of established and approved parameters.

It must be remembered that a delicate balance exist when interacting with children and young people. Too frequently it is reported that an adult has inappropriately interacted with a child or young person. In some instances the problem is simply a matter of perception, but even in those instances the damage caused is more often than not irreversible and usually it was avoidable.

While it is important to establish close relationships with children and young people when working to positively affect them, it is more important to establish those relationships properly.

Twenty

"We got rules, old rules and some new rules. Our rules are no different than y'all rules, they are our rules."
Byron Willson, age 86

10 Key Strategies for Urban Youth Culture Engagement

1. Be yourself; be consistently calm, happy, positive and real. You do not have to be a Jay-Z, Missy Elliott or Tupac Shakur to relate to young people.

2. Never react to behavior that is designed to be confrontational and obviously evoke an emotional and/or negative reaction. Pause and consider the purpose of the behavior, what's the real cause? After quickly considering and assessing the causes then respond in the appropriate fashion. With some young people, knee jerk reaction to their behaviors is exactly what they're looking for; they're trying to discover which of your buttons they can push. Observe and think before responding, and remember, try not to react emotionally or negatively, but always respond.

3. Have an open door for communication. Sincere dialogue is critical to establishing and maintaining meaningful relationships with youth.

4. Have some knowledge of Youth Culture. Know something about young people and the things that are important to them.

5. If you are not connecting, pass off to someone who can effectively represent you. Sometimes it is just not clicking, in these instances have another person (young or old) who has their respect, and understands their language and symbols communicate with them on your behalf.

6. Consider and try to understand their point, even if you don't agree. Avoid falling into the trap of being disrespectful and/or dismissive of their views.

7. Peace is reflected in peace. Stay positive, if things are turning negative, you can pass off to another person, or change the subject, but avoid allowing negativity to overcome the situation by any means necessary.

8. At the right time have an exchange of youth and adult culture points. What do they know about you? What do you know about them? Share this moment individually and collectively.

9. Pizza & Pop…try to have real sit-down moments with food and refreshments. A great method to get positive results is to play each other's music and movies, engage in games and other activities together. Agree on the activities and entertainment beforehand.

10. Keep the relationship honest, don't fake it and don't front. If you sense strains in the relationship, address them at the appropriate time. Use technology: e-mail, cell phones and whatever else can assist you in keeping your relationship positive and progressive.

Twenty-one

"We hear old school say the same old things & do nuthing...on the other hand young fellas have attitudes all the time."
James, age 19

Positive Urban Youth Development
PUYD

It is recognized that there are a host of very valuable, well respected and well established doctrines and schools of thought regarding positive youth development. While many of the concepts and theorems are applicable to urban youth and the challenges they face, until recently there has been no one approach designed specifically to address the needs of the urban community and its children and youth. In light of this fact a new approach is being constructed that takes into consideration the factors and variables that are specific to the urban ecology and its diverse nature.

A primary goal of Positive Urban Youth Development (PUYD) is exposure. The primary method for achieving this goal is through the use of experiential learning situations. The secondary method for achieving this goal is through adult engagement of and interaction with community children and youth. For the child or young person growing up in disenfranchised communities it is critical that they are motivated to achieve and succeed socially, educationally and/or vocationally.

Not all children and young people growing up urban are at risk of failing to become an active participant in society, but recent trends reveal an astonishing rate of young people that are seceding from society as traditionally defined and commonly known. Lack of access or desire to access available educational and employment resources predisposes many young people from urban communities to lives that will fail to establish adequate legitimate methods to provide for themselves and their families.

If the modern urban youth is to compete in the ever growing, developing and increasingly complex global society of today they must develop in ways that allow them to compete with not only their urban peers and suburban counterparts and peers but also their counterparts throughout the globe. Exposure to both the challenges and opportunities facing the urban youth is the first step to providing the child and adolescent that is growing up urban in the modern world with the necessary tools for positive development and growth.

The children and young people growing urban up often have access to opportunities that are outside of acceptable (oftentimes legal and legitimate) resources. This fact must be recognized and understood if inroads are to be made into effectively engaging children and young people growing and developing in urban communities. The tendency to ignore or "brush off" the significance of these "opportunities" that urban youth have access to is not only foolhardy but detrimental to the professional or volunteer working to positively affect this particular group of children and young people.

The Positive Urban Youth Development Model is designed around a group of key concepts; these include but are not limited to the following:

Key Concepts of Positive Urban Youth Development

1) Expand the horizons of each child and young person.

2) Reveal the possibilities available.

3) Connect to the community (point out assets & liabilities).

4) Develop cultural competence.

5) Connect with community elders.

Strategies for practical application of key concepts

1) **Expand their horizons:** Watch videos about other places; movies that contain historical facts

about their own community and the world around them are useful tools. Engage in discussion about the world outside of their immediate environment/communities. Go on field trips whenever possible to any locations that provide the opportunities for new and expanded experiences and dialogue regarding such experiences.

Take every opportunity to engage the child or young person in discussion about their community and what exist in the world beyond it.

2) **Reveal the possibilities:** Point out and stress the skills and abilities that each child or young person you interact with possesses. Reveal their strengths; discuss areas for potential growth. Uncover hidden assets on a personal level and those that might exist in the community. Talk whenever possible about personal, family and community assets. Point out and talk about obstacles and challenges. Examine those things that might seem to present stumbling blocks, discuss methods for approaching, avoiding or overcoming them. Discuss the importance of facing challenges when appropriate and avoiding potential threats, danger and avoidable situations and/or circumstances.

3) **Connect to the community:** Connect community youth and children to their environment by involving them in programs and projects that establish a

sense of community history and pride. Work with organizations and programs in the community to provide children and youth the opportunity to connect to all of the positive assets in their personal eco-systems. Explore the environment to discover and discuss the natural world and its role in the community. Interact with churches, schools, social agencies, businesses and other youth groups in the community in an effort to engage children and young people as stake holders and owners of their homeland community and those nearby communities that are neighbors. By connecting to people and places within their own community and surrounding communities youth will discover a vast array of new friendships, potential opportunities, new ideas and resources otherwise likely to remain undiscovered.

4) **Develop cultural competence:** Encourage cultural competence and acceptance by helping develop an appreciation for cultural diversity among community youth. Promote use of technology to provide young people with the opportunity to connect with other young people from other cultures. Arrange for programs and projects with young people from other cultures, religions and ethnicities. Encourage dialogue about cultural differences and the positive contributions of people from all cultures, religions and ethnicities in the world. Have programs that offer food and entertainment from different cultures.

5) **Connect with community elders:** Connect community youth with their elders in the community by establishing programs to engage the young and old in recreational activities, educational/mentoring opportunities and dialogue. Have children and young people participate in programs assisting the elderly, being tutored by retired adults in educational and vocational studies. Establish networks for exchanging information, ideas and needs between children, youth and adults within the community. Such systems might include community message boards or systems that provide for individuals to post help wanted positions to be checked by people looking to provide assistance. An aggressive approach to aligning elders and young people in a cycle of progressive, productive dialogue and engagement has tremendous potential for alignment and use of extraordinary community resources.

Expected Outcomes of PUYD

1) Demonstrable Positive Role Modeling Continuum

2) Demonstrable Positive Peer Influence

3) Demonstrable Positive Decision Making

4) Demonstrable Social Competencies

5) DemonstrableEducational/Vocational Progress

1) Positive role model establishment is a reciprocal relationship process whereby adults in the community assume roles as primary models of positive responsible behavior. This behavior is continually reinforced as community youth are expected to reciprocate by behaving in a positive, responsible fashion as is expected of all members of the community. In this behavioral continuum each member of the community reinforces the concepts of proper and expected behavior. Elders encourage and motivate younger members of the community with positive behaviors and attitudes being established as the expected norm.

2) As with the positive role model continuum, the establishment of the positive peer influence continuum relies on the constant participation of all members of the communal group. Those individuals that are recognized as leaders among groups are at the forefront of the vanguard that carries the mantle for positive peer influence. Positive peer influence is most effective when positive results are evident. Indications of progress might include but not be limited to: Praise for jobs and tasks well done, rewards in the form of formal acknowledgement, prizes, awards, payment for jobs and tasks, etc. The more members of the collective become aware that there is benefit to positive attitudes and behaviors the easier it becomes to affect the positive peer influence continuum.

3) Positive decisions yield positive results. This fact must be demonstrated to have permanent results that build self esteem and confidence among urban youth. Destroying the myth that the "hood" is inescapable, or that there is positive gain from negative activity, attitude and behavior is a process that requires constant denunciation of urban myth, lies and lore. Continual reinforcement of the benefits of practice and persistence will ultimately give rise to belief in a beneficial approach to making progress regardless of where one begins to work to affect positive change in their lives and their communities.

4) The inability or lack of understanding regarding the basic competencies necessary for functioning in the world is cause for frustration among many in America (young and old) and throughout the world. The child or young person that recognizes that he or she is limited because they do not possess the knowledge and understanding of how to behave or speak in a particular environment is reason for many to not pursue opportunities that might exist for them. Additionally it is noted that recognition of limitations and inabilities is cause for resentment among an extraordinarily large segment of society. Developing social competencies is critical to the positive development of urban children and youth. Allowing young people to learn with no fear of humiliation or ridicule provides a benefit to not only the young person involved but has far reaching

benefit to the larger community and society. Beyond the basics of reading, writing and communication skills it is important that young people learn basics regarding team work, interviewing for jobs, basic etiquette, dressing for work, etc.

5) Helping the urban child and young person to discover their talents and aptitude for career opportunities is a critical component of PUYD. Recognition that there is nobility in every form of legal and legitimate employment is a primary component of the PUYD model. Young people must be encouraged to utilize every skill and ability they possess and then they must be assisted in discovering those resources available that will help them in the proper training, education and development of skills that will ultimately help them in the pursuit of gainful employment and career opportunities. It cannot be stressed enough that the value of those jobs and careers that require vocational training, apprenticeships and other types of training and/or learning processes that do not require a college education are valued just as those are that require college and advanced degrees.

Indicators of Progress

1) Youth become community resources.

2) Youth are empowered to contribute to the community and to be part of community solutions and problem solving.

3) Youth provide valuable community services (volunteerism).

4) The community becomes asset based and focused.

5) Community youth, adults and elders develop a partnership continuum that establishes a natural progress cycle.

The Asset Based Community

The asset based community recognizes and supports a progress continuum reliant on the perpetuation and continuation of all of its positive elements for its vitality, growth and continued success. In the asset based community each citizen is an integral component necessary to the very existence of each member of the community, it is therefore recognized that the whole is equal to all of its parts. The successes and/or failures of any member of the community are acknowledged as part of the success and/or failure of the entire community. It is therefore critical to ensure that each member of the community achieve the most possible in order that the entire collective (whole of community citizenry) might benefit to the fullest extent possible. This concept is the basic premise of the democratic system and should be effectively applied in all communities, it is essential to the continued existence and survival of urban communities.

The three primary components of the asset based community are:
1) Community youth gain life skills, jobskills/ training and education.

2) The community continually creates economic opportunities.

3) The community establishes and maintains a progressive cycle of continual improvement.

If the modern urban community is to remain vital, if urban communities are to remain an integral part of broader communities, if society as established is to survive then it is critical that the urban ecology be reinvigorated. In many instances throughout Urban America and in urban communities throughout the world the development of a third polity has taken root. The hybrid urban subculture and eco-system that denounces traditional ways and means and that exist only for the perpetuation of itself and the exploitation of the denizens of its community is now well established.

Modern children and youth are prey for a culture that unchecked will consume them as it continues to grow, mutate and ultimately destroy those communities it manages to negatively affect. The asset based community, that community that reinvents itself by reclaiming its children and youth and recognizing its assets and resources is the salvation for those growing up urban and for all urban communities.

Twenty-two

"There is life beyond our neighborhood; you just need somebody to help you find it."
Jamal, age 20

Best Practices

The Act for Youth Upstate Center of Excellence comprised a list of Best Practices for Youth Development Programs. These suggestions are designed to offer parents; policy makers, program, community, and school leader's supportive information that will help youth build new skills, and develop positive relationships with adults and peers:

• **Comprehensive, long-term programs that involve all aspects of a young person's life, home, school, and community:**
A comprehensive, multi-faceted approach that addresses the teens themselves, their families, peer groups, schools, neighborhood, community, society, and the media allows for reinforcement of new skills and knowledge in several different contexts. Programs should work in meaningful partnerships with other community institutions, such as schools, and should continue over time to allow participants to complete important activities, as well as reinforce the program goals and objectives.

• **Strong relationships with parents/other adults:**
Involvement of parents and caregivers reinforce what youth are learning and create opportunities for family communication on teen issues. In addition to

189

family support, youth also benefit from a one-on-one caring relationship with another adult who is warm, friendly, accepting, affirming, shows interest, and is also easily approachable and accessible.

• **New roles and responsibilities for youth:**
Youth should be offered diverse and quality experiences in order to gain and develop skills that directly relate to their future goals (including career objectives). Youth should be connected to resources that provide them with opportunities and support to help them reach these goals. These opportunities should encourage youth to play meaningful leadership roles and contribute their talents.

• **Attention to specific youth needs in a physically and psychologically safe environment:**
Effective programs and strategies are housed in a safe environment and are age specific, developmentally appropriate, and culturally sensitive.

• **Highly qualified and diverse staff that are well trained and committed to the youth development philosophy:**
Staff should have sufficient training and experience to teach and lead. They should believe in the program, be committed to the positive development of youth, and specifically the avoidance of "adultism" or presuming that youth are inferior to adults because of their lack of age and experience.

• **Opportunities for critical thinking and active, self-directed learning:**
This process involves youth gathering information from different sources and experiences, drawing their own meaning from it, and expressing the implications of what they have newly learned to themselves and others. New roles and responsibilities coupled with time for reflection can provide youth with these opportunities.

• **Programs that motivate and convey high expectations for youth:**
Youth benefit from programs that provide structure and predictability, that is, when there are clear rules and standards that are guided and monitored.

• **Teach specific skills using interactive teaching methods:**
The use of interactive teaching methods such as discussion groups personalizes the information and encourages youth engagement in setting their own developmental goals. Programs should provide models, as well as opportunities to practice communication, negotiation, and refusal skills.

Information on best practices was obtained from (Cornell University, University of Rochester, & New York Center for School Safety 2003)

Twenty-three

"Young people need positive experiences. If we had not been exposed to other positive experiences we would not have been successful in our adult life."
Rev. Floyd David Smith

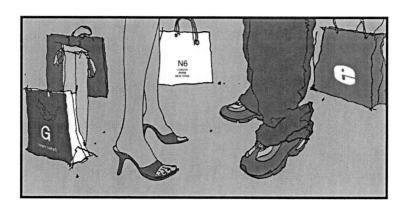

Conclusion

Urban youth represent a significant part of the future of America, the challenges they face and their ultimate successes and failures will inevitably impact all of society. In a global society that finds distance more and more meaningless it has been discovered that the influence of urban youth is creating much in the way of dynamic change in youth culture throughout the globe.

Those devoted to working with urban children, youth and families are in the unique position to have real positive impact on the world of tomorrow.

In Greek mythology a curious Pandora opened the box entrusted to her by the gods, with this deed all of the ills of humanity escaped into the realm, leaving behind only hope which remained in its place. Urban communities in many instances are akin to Pandora's Box, the lid to the contents have been slowly pried open over the last century. Today the children of urban communities face challenges impossible to have foreseen not so long ago. Perhaps through negligence, likely through ignorance and apathy an eco-system has evolved in urban communities that can be harsh, brutal and unforgiving.

There are those that would diminish the harsh realities of growing up urban or as street vernacular would say "in the hood." For the detractors it is suggested that they take the time to closely look at the urban landscape and examine just how dangerous and destructive it has become in recent years.

Of course there are elements of urban communities and urban living that are the exception but here we are addressing the very real negative aspect (street culture) that is having such a disastrous effect on young people now and unchecked will inevitably negatively impact future generations as well. There is no question that urban centers throughout America are turning out scores of talented, well-adjusted, contributing members of society. It is noted however that there are detrimental elements that have become more prevalent that impede the progress of all children and young people growing up in their midst. Additionally it is noted that it is inexcusable and unforgivable to have one child lost to the ills that so frequently claim our young.

For the professional and the volunteer working with urban children, youth and families it is imperative that one be familiar with the dynamics associated with urban communities. Street culture is a major aspect of urban living and must be recognized for the influence it has on the attitudes and behavior of urban youth. The ability to understand street lingo, hip-hop culture, the signs and symbols so intricately entwined in urban culture is a vital skill.

As evidenced earlier hip-hop is the pre-dominant culture of urban youth but it is noted that not all urban youth subscribe to hip-hop philosophy, ideology or doctrine. Additionally it is noted that hip-hop culture as with most aspects of pop culture is not monolithic. What's most important is for the person working with urban youth to recognize and respect the culture that is embraced by the youth they are working with. This is not to suggest that every aspect of a specific culture must be embraced by the professional or volunteer, merely that they be knowledgeable and that they restrain themselves from aggressively displaying any misgivings they may have regarding the music or relative culture.

Obviously it is not suggested that there be any tolerance for vulgarity, misogyny, violence, pornography or any other negative aspect of any form of music, entertainment or culture. In many instances such negative aspects of a culture or form of expression can be positively challenged and subsequently exposed for their negative and usually detrimental nature.

Understanding urban youth, appreciating them for their uniqueness and their abilities and then working to positively affect and motivate them will yield tremendous benefit to those interacting with them, for the young people themselves and for the community.

Reference
Page

References

2004 Profile of HIV/AIDS: The Detroit Metro Area. (2004). Retrieved December 1, 2004, from http://www.michigan.gov/documents/Det_EMA_text_and_tables_104208_7.pdf

Acoca, L. (1999). Investing in girls: A 21st strategy. Juvenile Justice Journal, VI(1).

Brooks, G. (1960). We real cool. In The bean eaters. New York: Harpers.

Byrd, A., & Solomon, A. (2005). The mix: Take back the music. Essence, 82-86.

Campbell, A. (1984). The Girls in the Gang. New York: Basil Blackwell.

Center for Disease Control. (2004). Youth violence: Fact sheet. Retrieved December 12, 2004, from http://www.cdc.gov/ncipc/factsheets/yvfacts.htm

Chesney-Lind, M. (1999). Girls, Gangs and Violence. In M. Chesney-Lind & J. M. Hagedorn (Eds.), Female Gangs in America. Chicago: Lake View Press.

Children's Defense Fund. (2001). Retrieved August 8, 2002, 2001, from http://www.childrensdefense.org/release010417.htm

Cornell University, University of Rochester, & New York Center for School Safety (2003). Research facts and findings: Best practices for youth develpment programs, from http://www.actforyouth.net/documents/may_factsheet
_web.pdf

Deschenes, E. P. (1999). Violence among girls: Does gang membership make a difference? In M. Chesney-Lind & J. M. Hagedorn (Eds.), Female Gangs in America. Chicago: Lake View Press.

Editors. (2005). The mix: Take back the music. Essence, 82.

Erkut, S., Fields, J. P., Sing, R., & Marx, F. (1996). Diversity in girls' experiences: Feeling good about who you are. In B. J. R. Leadbeater & N. Way (Eds.), Urban girls: Resisting stereotypes, creating identities (pp. 53-64). New York: New York University Press.

Frankel, L. (2003). Research facts and findings: Self esteem. Retrieved November 2, 2004, from http://www.actforyouth.net/documents/june_self_esteem.pdf

Hall, W. (2004, 4/27). Violence among girls catches some off guard. Detroit News, p. 3A.

HIV/AIDS and minority women. (2004). Retrieved December 7, 2004, from http://www.omhrc.gov/hivaidsobservances/fs/04-1013Women.pdf

Houser, D., Pooh, D. J., & Worrall, J. (2004). Grand theft auto: San andreas. US: Rockstar Games [us].

Jargowsky, P. A. (1997). The face of poverty: Family and schooling in America's slums, ghettos, and barrios. Retrieved December 23, 2004, from http://www.children.smartlibrary.org/NewInterface/segment.cfm?segment=1826&table_of_contents=1505

Perry-Botinger, L. (2004). Obesity & African American Women. Retrieved December 7, 2004, from http://www.heartcenteronline.com

Shorter-Gooden, K., & Washington, N. C. (1996). Young black, and female: The challenge of weaving an identity. Journal of Adolescence, 19, 465-475.

Skillman Center for Children, College of Urban, Labor and Metropolitan Affairs, Wayne State University;

Institutute for Social Research University of Michigan, and members of the Wayne County Female Services Advisory Committee. (2002). The Signs Are There: Girls and Juvenile Justice in Wayne

County. Detroit: Skillman Center for Children.

Smith-Minifee, P. (2004). Positive youth development of African American adolescent females who reside in an urban community. Michigan State University, East Lansing.

Snyder, H. N., & Sickmund, M. (1999). Juvenile offenders and victims: 1999 national report. Washington, D.C.: Office of Juvenile Justice and Delinquency Prevention, U.S. Department of Justice.

Stevens, J. W. (1997). African American female adolescent identity development: A three dimensional perspective. Child Welfare, 76(1), 145-172.

Talking, F. a. (2003). What are body images and self-esteem? Retrieved December 20, 2004, from http://www.siecus.org/pubs/ families/FAT_Newsletter_V2N4.pdf

Taylor, C. S. (1993). Girls, gangs, women, and drugs. East Lansing: Michigan State University Press.

Taylor, R. J., Tucker, M. B., Chatters, L. M., & Jayakody, R. (1997). Recent demographic trends in African American family structure. In R. J. Taylor, L. M. Chatters & R. Jayakody (Eds.), Family Life in Black America. Thousand Oaks: Sage Publication.

Tolman, D. L. (1996). Adolescent girls' sexuality: Debunking the myth of the urban girl. In B. J. R. Leadbeater & N. Way (Eds.), Urban girl: Resisting stereotypes, creating identities (pp. 255-271). New York and London: New York University Press.

Wilson, W. J. (2000). Youth violence in urban communities. Cambridge: Harvard University.

Made in the USA